Longing

ased on two short stories by Anton Chekhov

With an introduction by Donald Rayfield

Methuen Drama

Introduction copyright © Donald Rayfield 2013

British Library Cataloguing-in-Publication Data
A catalogue record for this book is available from the British Library.

ISBN: PB: 978-1-4725-1745-6
ePub: 978-1-4725-1743-2
ePDF: 978-1-4725-1744-9

Typeset by Mark Heslington Ltd, Scarborough, North Yorkshire
Printed and bound in Great Britain

Anton Chekhov – An Alphabet

Anton. Anton Chekhov died nearly a hundred and nine years ago, on July 15th 1904. He was forty-four years old. His lungs were ravaged by tuberculosis. In Russia Chekhov is revered as a short story writer of genius and his plays are considered as extremely interesting but somehow ancillary and complimentary to his main achievement. And this Russian conception of his work has some validity: Chekhov, whatever his standing as a playwright, is quite probably the best short story writer ever. Like certain great pieces of music, his stories repay constant revisitings. The two dozen or so mature stories he wrote in the last decade of the 19th century have not dated: what resonated in them for his contemporaries resonates now, a hundred or more years on. Chekhov, it can be argued, was the first truly modern writer of fiction: secular, refusing to pass judgement, cognisant of the absurdities of our muddled, bizarre lives and the complex tragi-comedy that is the human condition.

Biarritz. Chekhov visited Biarritz in south-west France in 1897. His health was failing and he had to seek a warmer climate in the winter months. For an effectively monoglot Russian writer (scant French and a little German) and a semi-invalid he had travelled fairly far and wide in his life. In Europe he knew Germany, France and Italy (how one wishes he had visited England). In 1890 he made an epic eighty-day trans-Russian journey to Sakhalin, a prison island in furthest Siberia. The book he wrote about the conditions of the prisoners there is earnest but dull; it does not live up to the near intolerable struggle it took to reach the place. He came home by steamer via the orient: Hong Kong, Singapore, Ceylon and then through the Suez Canal to Odessa.

Critics. "Critics," Chekhov said once to Maxim Gorky, "are like horse-flies which prevent the horse from ploughing. The horse works, all its muscles drawn tight like the strings on a double bass and a fly settles on its flanks and tickles and buzzes . . . he has to twitch his skin and swish his tail. And what does the fly buzz about? It scarcely knows itself; simply because it is restless and wants to proclaim: 'Look I am living on the earth. See, I can buzz too, buzz about anything'." Chekhov went on: "For twenty-five years I have read criticisms of my stories and I don't remember a single remark of any value or one word of valuable advice. Only once [a critic] said something which made an impression on me – he said I would die in a ditch, drunk."

Drink. Untypically for a Russian of his era, Chekhov was not a heavy drinker. His elder brothers Kolia and Aleksandr were chronic alcoholics and perhaps the memory of the squalor of Kolia's wasted life (he was a hugely talented painter who died aged thirty-one) put Chekhov off. Yet Chekhov's last act in life was to drink a glass of champagne. Fatally ill, he had travelled to the German spa town of Badenweiler in the vain hope that German doctors might save him. German medical etiquette demanded that, when the patient was near death and there was nothing more that a doctor could do, a glass of champagne would be offered. Chekhov knew what this meant. He accepted the glass, muttered "*Ich sterbe*" ["I'm dying"] and drank it down. His last words were: "I haven't had champagne for a long time." Then he died.

Event-Plot. This is William Gerhardie's phrase – one he uses to describe the kind of fiction written before Chekhov. Gerhardie, who is tremendously acute about Chekhov (he published a passionately enthusiastic short book about him in 1924) spoke with real authority. An Englishman, born in Moscow in 1895, wholly bilingual, Gerhardie idolised Chekhov (whom he read in Russian long before he was translated). Gerhardie himself was described in his 1920s heyday as "the English Chekhov" and they do share a similar philosophy of life – though Gerhardie's talent had a briefer flowering. Gerhardie's analysis of Chekhov's genius maintains that for the first time in literature the fluidity and randomness of life was made the *form* of the fiction.

Previous to Chekhov, the event-plot drove all fictions: the narrative was manipulated, tailored, calculatedly designed, rounded-off. Tolstoy, Flaubert, Dickens and Turgenev could not resist the event-plot powering and shaping their novels. Chekhov abandoned this type of self-conscious "story" for something more casual and realistic. As Gerhardie says, Chekhov's stories are "blurred, interrupted, mauled or otherwise tampered with by life". This is why Chekhov's stories still speak to us a hundred years on. His stories are anti-novelistic, in the traditional sense. They are like life as we all live it.

Faith. Chekhov's personal world was a godless one: despite his orthodox religious upbringing, he asserted, in 1892, that "I have no religion now". He wrote about religious folk, indeed one of his greatest stories is entitled "The Bishop". But intelligent people who believed in God seemed baffling to him. "I squandered away my faith long ago and never fail to be puzzled by an intellectual who is also a believer."

Grigorovitch. In 1886 Dmitri Grigorovitch, a distinguished Russian writer, wrote Chekhov a letter which changed his artistic life. Up until that date Chekhov had earned his living as a composer of humorous short stories, almost like variety sketches (he was a qualified doctor but it was his writing that sustained him financially). He published these *jeux d'esprits* under a pseudonym, "Antosha Chekhonte". The vast majority of them have not aged well: arch, knowing, manifestly trying to be funny, these stories were hack-work. Then in 1886 he published a story, "Requiem" under his own name. Grigorovitch was hugely impressed, and wrote to Chekhov acclaiming his talent and urging him to abandon his comic squibs. "Stop doing hack-work . . . better go hungry . . . save up your impressions for work that has been pondered, polished, written at several sittings." Chekhov was overwhelmed by this letter and his reply is valuable if only because it is perhaps the only time that Chekhov drops his guard and gushes. "Your letter struck me like lightning. I almost burst into tears, I was profoundly moved and I now feel it has left a deep trace in my soul." Grigorovitch's passionate urging worked. For Chekhov it was a Damascene moment. The fifteen years remaining to him bear witness to his new zeal as a serious artist.

Home. Chekhov was born in 1860, in a town called Taganrog, far to the south of Moscow on the Sea of Azov. More Levantine than European (Turkey was 300 miles away), Taganrog was a hot, fly-infested port with a varied population – Russians, Greeks, Armenians, Italians. Chekhov's father was an indigent grocer whose debts eventually caused the family to flee to Moscow. Chekhov had four brothers and one sister – Aleksandr, Kolia, Vania, Misha and Masha. Very early in his life Chekhov became the family breadwinner. He supported them all – doggedly and in the main ungrudgingly – until his death.

Intimacy. In his short life Chekhov had many lovers but he had, as we would now term it, a real problem with commitment. Most of the women he had affairs with would have been happy to marry him but Chekhov was always careful to keep them at a distance, to break the relationship off if it seemed likely to become too heated.

The Japanese girl. In his travels in the Russian Far East, on his way to Sakhalin, Chekhov went to a brothel in Blagoveshchensk. He wrote to a friend, "The Japanese girl . . . doesn't put on airs, or go coy, like a Russian woman. And all the time she is laughing and making lots of *tsu* noises . . . When you come, the Japanese girl pulls with her teeth a sheet of cotton wool from her sleeve, catches you by the "boy", gives you a massage and the cotton wool tickles your belly. All this is done with coquetry, laughing, singing and saying *tsu*."

Koumiss. A fermented mare's milk that was believed, in the 1890s, to be a defence against tuberculosis, as a source of "good" bacilli. In 1901 Ckekhov undertook a koumiss cure, drinking four bottles of the milk daily. He gained twelve pounds in weight in a fortnight. A month later he was still coughing blood.

Lika Mizinova – the one true love of Chekhov's life? Chekhov married the actress Olga Knipper in 1901 when he had three years left to live. It was a union that dumbfounded and outraged most of his family – it seemed incomprehensible. It has subsequently been presented as one of the great romances of the 20th century. My own theory is that his long affair with Lika Mizinova was the real love story. He met Lika in 1889, she was a teacher, an aspiring opera singer, blonde and buxom and nineteen years old. Chekhov was ten years older. For almost a decade they conducted a bantering, passionate on-off love affair. No other woman in Chekhov's life held his affections so long but he always refrained from proposing marriage. Frustrated, Lika had an affair with Chekhov's close friend and business manager Ignati Potapenko (a married man). They had a child together. Betrayal enough to break up any relationship, one would have thought – but Chekhov kept seeing Lika. Her career failed, she grew plump but something kept drawing him back to her. They last met in 1897 but Lika remained very friendly with Chekhov's brothers and sister. She is often considered to be the model for Nina in *The Seagull*.

"My Life". This is the longest story Chekhov wrote, it's almost a novella and is, in my opinion, his greatest. In it you will find all the key Chekhovian tropes: the black humour, the candid depiction of the absurdity of life, its fleeting happiness, its "weirdness and vulgarity" (as Stanislavsky put it), its brutal randomness. This dark Chekhovian comic ruthlessness found its way into English literature via William Gerhardie. Katherine Mansfield plagiarised Chekhov but she responded to his more elegiac tone. Gerhardie sensed Chekhov's tough realism, his acknowledgement of life's bland cruelty. Gerhardie in turn was a huge influence on Evelyn Waugh (Waugh's early comedies are extremely Gerhardian, a fact that Waugh himself acknowledged later in life). This tone of voice has subsequently come to seem very English, but it was there in Chekhov first. My other favourite Chekhov stories in no particular order are: The Lady with the Dog, In the Ravine, A Visit to Friends, Ionych, The Bishop, The House with the Mezzanine, Three Years.

Nice. Chekhov went to Nice in 1898 to protect his damaged lungs from the ravages of the Russian winter. It's a city I know well, I spent most of a year there in 1971. Like Biarritz, Nice is a place where, here and there, the ghost of Chekhov haunts its streets. At the turn of the century it was popular with Russians and Chekhov stayed in a Russian pension in the rue Gounod. The room I rented was on the rue Dante, a few blocks away. Chekhov liked Nice (the weather was good) and tolerated the routine and circumscribed life he lived there. Nice was a good place to read, he said, but not to write.

Olga Knipper was a leading actress at the Moscow Art Theatre. She acted in the earliest productions of Chekhov's four finished plays – *The Seagull*, *Uncle Vanya*, *Three Sisters* and *The Cherry Orchard*. Chekhov married her in 1901, three years before he died. Olga survived him by 55 years, dying in 1959 (She also survived Hitler and Stalin). She was an ardent keeper of the flame but, despite her efforts to portray it otherwise, there is no disguising that the marriage was a strange one. They spent much more time apart than together (hence their copious and affecting correspondence): she acting in Moscow, Chekhov convalescing in Yalta on the Black Sea. Sometimes she even kept her Moscow address from her husband. She and Chekhov tried to conceive a child but failed. There is strong evidence, however, that she was unfaithful to him and miscarried another lover's child in 1902.

Pavel Egerovitch Chekhov, Chekhov's father. The son of a serf, he was both absurdly devout and a ruthless disciplinarian. He beat his sons remorselessly. Chekhov saw it as the watershed in his life the day he woke knowing that he would not be beaten by his father. Yet this sentimental, sadistic boor was financially supported loyally and tirelessly by his third son throughout his life, living with him in his various establishments and particularly at Melikhovo, the small estate Chekhov bought to the south of Moscow and which, of all the places he lived in (from 1892 to 1899), he most loved. Pavel Chekhov effectively ran the estate with shrewd serf-like application. He died in 1898, aged seventy-three, on an operating table when the surgeon was attempting to rectify a gangrenous hernia. Pavel had forgotten to put on his truss and developed the fatal hernia by picking up a 20 lb bag of sugar. Chekhov declared it the end of an era, that "the main cog had jumped out of the Melikhovo machine". He never loved his father but he had never let him down. He abandoned Melikhovo shortly after his father died.

Quinine. At Melikhovo Chekhov had two dachshunds which he called Quinine and Bromine. Quinine was his favourite. The most natural and unposed photographs of Chekhov show him sitting on the steps of his veranda with Quinine tucked under his arm. When he was obliged to leave Melikhovo and go and live in the Crimea, because of his tuberculosis, the dachshunds were left behind. Bromine was shot as a rabies suspect and Quinine was torn to pieces by feral dogs.

Real lives. Chekhov said: "Every person lives his real, most interesting life under the cover of secrecy". By this I take him to mean that other people are fundamentally opaque, mysterious – even people you know very well, your wife or husband, your family. Janet Malcolm, who has written an intriguing book on Chekhov (called *Reading Chekhov*), says that "We never see people in life as clearly as we see the people in novels, stories and plays; there is a veil between ourselves and even our closest intimates, blurring us to each other." This, it seems to me, is the great and lasting allure of all fiction: if we want to know what other people are like we turn to the novel or the short story. In no other art form can we take up residence in other people's minds so effortlessly. Chekhov tells us a great deal about his characters but, however, resists full exposure: there always remains something "blurry", something secret about them. This is part of his genius: this is what makes his stories seem so real.

Aleksei Suvorin. A vastly wealthy, right-wing publisher and newspaper magnate and probably Chekhov's closest male friend. Chekhov achieved a bond with Suvorin which is hard to explain, given the latter's rebarbative politics. It's rather as if George Orwell's best friend had been, say, Julius Streicher. I suspect Suvorin functioned as something of a surrogate father for Chekhov (he was twenty years older) – also he paid him well and Chekhov's fame largely came about through his stories appearing in Suvorin's publications. Suvorin had no illusions about Chekhov: ". . . a man of flint and a cruel talent with his harsh objectivity. He's spoilt, his *amour propre* is enormous." They fell out, finally, irrevocably, over the Dreyfus affair. Chekhov was an ardent Dreyfusard; Suvorin unashamedly anti-Semitic. There was no real rapprochement and Suvorin bitterly regretted the rift. Asked about his politics once, Chekhov declared that he wanted only to be a "free artist". Like Vladimir Nabokov, he was deeply distrustful of fiction that openly proselytised for any political ideology. Chekhov's view of the human condition, given his own terminal illness, was bleakly clear-eyed. "After youth comes old age; after happiness, unhappiness, and vice versa; nobody can be healthy and cheerful all their lives . . . you have to be ready for anything. You just have to do your duty as best as you can."

Theatre. Chekhov was both drawn to and exasperated by the theatre. He wrote his first plays purely as a way of making quick money. One always feels that he was somewhat amazed at the acclaim his later plays achieved. Seen in the light of the mature stories, the plays are clearly heavily indebted to the fiction in their mood, themes and settings – which is what made them so revolutionary and, later on, so influential. But the plays lack the seamless authority of the fiction: there are great characters, wonderful scenes, tremendous passages, moments of acute melancholy and sagacity but the parts appear greater than the whole. Perhaps only in *The Cherry Orchard* does everything fuse and the drama takes on an autonomy of its own. Days before his death he conceived the idea for a play about passengers stranded on an ice-bound ship. Perhaps his premature death makes the plays that Chekhov never wrote the real loss. The stories are fully achieved: a genuine apotheosis.

Uncle Vanya. Tolstoy went to see *Uncle Vanya* and loathed it. Chekhov was back stage and asked what Tolstoy's opinion was. A kindly interlocutor said that the great man hadn't "really understood" the play. Chekhov saw through that one. But then Tolstoy told him that, "You know I can't stand Shakespeare's plays, but yours are even worse." Chekhov found this delightfully, hilariously amusing.

Vanity. Chekhov was six foot one inches tall – a very tall man for the end of the 19th century. He was handsome: in early photos he looks burly and strangely asiatic. The familiar images of his last decade, goateed, with pince nez, slimmed by his illness, carefully dressed, testify to a man who was proud of his appearance and knew he was attractive to women. He had a terror of going bald.

Writers. Chekhov wrote in a letter to Suvorin, "Remember, that writers whom we call great or just good and who make us drunk have one common, very important feature: they are going somewhere and calling you with them, and you feel not with your mind, but your whole being, that they have a goal, like the ghost of Hamlet's father." He also said: "Writers must be as objective as a chemist."

X-rays. An X-ray of Chekhov's lungs early in his life (had such a thing been available) would have shown the shadowy traces of the "tubercules": latent walled-in lesions of the bacillus *Mycobacterium tuberculosis*. Chekhov probably caught the disease in childhood. And he saw his brother Kolia die of it in 1889. Moreover, Chekhov was a doctor: he knew exactly what was in store for him. The bacilli lie dormant in the body, kept at bay by the immune system. At moments when the immune system is under stress or weakened the bacilli break out of the tubercules and begin to spread extensively in the lungs. The lung tissue is then effectively eaten by the bacilli – *consumed* – hence the 19th century name for the disease: "consumption". In Chekhov's time – the pre-antibiotic era – the only cure was isolation, rest and good nutrition. In the last years of his life Chekhov's lungs became increasingly devastated. The amount of lung tissue available for the exchange of gases in the breathing process radically decreased. Chekhov died of breathing failure, exhaustion and general toxemia (the tuberculosis had also spread to the spine).

Yalta. A popular resort much favoured by tubercular patients. Positioned in the Crimea on the Black Sea it had a congenial climate. Chekhov moved there in 1899 and built a house, only returning to Moscow in the summer. The fact that he had taken up residence made the resort instantly chic – other invalids suddenly wanted to convalesce there rather than anywhere else – something that he doubtless found wryly amusing. His famous story 'The Lady with the Dog" is set in the town. Many of Yalta's transient lady visitors fancied themselves as the model for Anna, the eponymous heroine. Chekhov's Yalta house is now a museum, its furnishings and décor theoretically unchanged since Chekhov lived there.

Zoo. About a month before he died, the desperately ill Chekhov visited Moscow zoo. Chekhov loved animals. Apart from his dachshunds and the livestock on his estate he also had as pets two mongooses and, in Yalta, a tame crane. Conceivably, during that visit to Moscow zoo, Chekhov might have seen a cheetah in its cage. Donald Rayfield, Chekhov's best and definitive biographer, speculates that Chekhov's sexuality was like that of the cheetah. The male cheetah can only mate with a stranger. When the male cheetah mates with female cheetah familiar to him he is –

bizarrely – impotent. It's a fanciful image but one worth contemplating: the dying Chekhov staring at a cheetah in its cage. Perhaps this explains this rare man's extraordinary life and the view of the human condition that he refined in his incomparable stories. Perhaps it explains his enigmatic, beguiling personality: his convivial aloofness; his love of idleness; his immense generosity; his hard heart. For this artist to avoid impotence only strangers would do; it only worked with strangers. Anton Chekhov was a cheetah.

Introduction

By Donald Rayfield

The trouble with Chekhov's plays is that there are so few of them: four great plays (*Uncle Vanya, The Seagull, Three Sisters, The Cherry Orchard*), one good play, if carefully directed (*Ivanov*), and two impossible plays (the juvenile *Platonov*, and *The Wood Demon* the prototype of *Uncle Vanya*), plus a handful of fine, but conventional farces, and a few of Chekhov's own adaptations of short stories. Shakespeare, Ibsen, Molière or Ostrovsky have left dozens of major plays: even Aeschylus has bequeathed seven to posterity.

Why so few, especially when in 19th century Russia, as Chekhov himself admitted, a play was a pension? One reason is that Chekhov did not live long enough (although knowledge of impending death was perhaps his strongest source of inspiration); another was the resistance of the Russian theatre, until the very end of the century, to innovation; a third reason was Chekhov's dislike of actors and actresses, not as friends or mistresses, but as perverse and incompetent interpreters of his texts.

One successful device to overcome the paucity of original Chekhov's plays has been to exploit his adaptability, as great as Shakespeare's, to other times and locations: *Uncle Vanya* works as well in 20th-century New South Wales or Orkney; *The Cherry Orchard* can be reset in Somerset (John Fletcher's *The Apple Orchard*), Ireland (John McDonagh's lost *Weeds*), the Appalachians (Hume Cronyn's and Susan Cooper's *Foxfire*), or even the heel of Italy (Lion Feuchtwanger's *The American, or the Disenchanted City*); even *Ivanov* works brilliantly in 1920s Thessalonica. But swelling Chekhov's dramatic oeuvre by adapting some of his twenty or thirty greatest stories has not worked well. The secret was known to Chekhov alone: he often recycled prose fiction as drama (*Three Sisters* uses material from 'The Bride', *Uncle Vanya* from 'A Dreary Story', 'Fortune' and 'Panpipes', *Cherry Orchard* from 'A Visit to Friends', for instance). From a playwright's point of view, Chekhov's major stories often seem to lack dialogue and abound in impression and evocation: the greatest, like 'The Lady with the Dog', thus make fine cinema, even ballet, but not drama.

William Boyd has tried a new approach: fusion instead of fission. Admittedly, something similar, but more primitive, has been tried before, notably Michael Frayn's and Rowan Atkinson's *The Sneeze* which strings seven early comic stories into one farce, or Brian Friel's integration of *Three Sisters* into a trilogy of plays. Boyd, however, presents us with an unprecedented thorough-going transformation of two major, mature Chekhov stories which to a less perceptive eye would seem to have nothing much in common. Boyd has taken 'My Life' of 1896, one of Chekhov's longest and richest stories, taken its core and impacted it on 'A Visit to Friends' of 1898, a mere 16 pages which Chekhov disdained so much that it is the only mature work he excluded from his *Collected Works* and has been overlooked by most of Chekhov's translators.

'My Life', as the title and its first-person narrative suggests, is one of the few stories which the reader is tempted to read autobiographically. Its geography is that of Taganrog, the southern town where Chekhov was born and went to school; the hero, Misail, is, like Chekhov, spiritually bruised, if not crippled by a tyrannical, hypocritical father. Like Chekhov, he tries his hand at running his estate and, unlike his friends, admires the peasants whom he helps for their awareness of right and wrong, despite their drunkenness and ingratitude. As Misail marries a woman whose heart and ambition are fixed on the stage, the story even seems to predict Chekhov's own not particularly happy marriage. Misail is far less clever and creative than his author, but his open-mindedness, his dislike of dogma and pretence are authorial. Furthermore, the story is so rich in characters, incidents and mood that it would be a natural choice if the reader were allowed only one story to take to a desert island. Yet, in some ways, it is an atypical Chekhov

story: for one thing, a woman dies, and in Chekhov's work
mortality is almost exclusively male.

Boyd has stripped 'My Life' of most of its characters:
Misail's sister, his doctor 'friend' who seduces his sister, his
shy woman admirer: he takes Misail, an architect's son who
has dropped out (perhaps the first middle-class drop-out
in modern literature) to become a roof painter, his foreman
the philosophical 'Radish', the flamboyant woman he is
inveigled into marrying (now renamed Kleopatra), and his
father-in-law Dolzhikov, the ruthless railway engineer and
land speculator, and moves these four ill-assorted characters
into the family setting of 'A Visit to Friends'.

Why did Chekhov disdain 'A Visit to Friends'? He wrote
it during a half-involuntary nine months spent in a hotel in
Nice, recovering from a severe tubercular haemorrhage,
and his periods abroad were incompatible, in his view,
with creativity; he wrote it for a strange international,
multilingual magazine *Cosmopolis* (to which Rudyard Kipling
and Anatole France also contributed). But the real reason
may be that 'A Visit to Friends' is the embryo of *The Cherry
Orchard*. Like Ranevskaya, Tania is about to lose the estate
where she and her family have always lived, thanks to
her husband's (late husband's, in the case of Ranevskaya)
profligacy; like Ranevskaya, instead of practical measures,
when the auctioneer's hammer is hovering over her, she
clumsily tries to arrange a profitable marriage for her
youngest sister (in Ranevskaya's case, her ward and her
daughter). Tania invites her girl friend's old flame, a
successful Moscow bachelor lawyer, only for the lawyer
(Misha in the story, Kolia in Boyd's adaptation) to baulk
at the trap and do a moonlit flight. Likewise, in *The Cherry
Orchard*, the businessman and former peasant also runs off
without making the proposal to the girl and thus obliging
himself to save the family finances.

There may be other reasons, possibly autobiographical,
for Chekhov suppressing 'A Visit to Friends': as a result its
potential has been neglected until now. By bringing in the
railway engineer Dolzhikov as the man who will buy the

estate from Tania and her husband and install Misail there with his daughter, Boyd has supplied the primitive force of Lopakhin, who gives *The Cherry Orchard* its driving energy. Like Lopakhin, Boyd's Dolzhikov torments the musicians at his party and, by his cunning coup at the auction, betrays the family he promised to save.

Longing is surprisingly faithful in spirit to Chekhov: Misail still goes ahead with the marriage that will bring him only misery, and Kolia runs off to catch the dawn train to Moscow rather than make a proposal to the lovely young Natasha. Conventional comedies end in marriage: Chekhov's comedies (and he insisted that even his most sombre plays were comedies) end in non-marriage. In other ways, too, *Longing* is a classic Chekhov comedy: as in all good saturnalia, the servants' world runs in parallel to their masters'. In *Uncle Vanya* or *The Seagull* we realise that the servants control the action: they hide revolvers and horses from their masters and thus block their escape routes; in *The Cherry Orchard* they parody the landowning class. And in *Longing* only Radish the painter remains unperturbed and undisappointed by the action.

Other dramatists will now be reading Chekhov's stories to choose suitable material for this sort of nuclear fusion: the dearth of Chekhovian drama may eventually be over.

Longing

Longing had its world premiere at the Hampstead Theatre on 28 February 2013. The cast and creative team were as follows:

Sergei	Alan Cox
Radish	Tom Georgeson
Kolia	Iain Glen
Varia	Tamsin Greig
Tania	Natasha Little
Natasha	Eve Ponsonby
Misail	William Postlethwaite
Olga / Mrs Luganovitch	Mary Roscoe
Dolzikhov	John Sessions
Kleopatra	Catrin Stewart

Director　Nina Raine
Designer　Lizzie Clachan
Lighting Designer　James Farncombe
Music　Patrick Doyle
Choreographer　Jane Gibson
Sound Designer　Gareth Fry
Casting Director　Amy Ball

Act One

Scene One

The stage is occupied by a somewhat broken down summer house set in the park of a provincial estate in Russia at the end of the 19th century. The paint is flaking, streaks of rust line the walls from the leaking gutters, the rooftiles are warped and sunbleached, the balustrade of the veranda has been patched up. Very shabby-genteel, but full of character.

The summer house is basically single storey but there is a small dormer window in the roof and it has a wide veranda with two doors giving on to it, numerous chairs and a table.

Around the summer house we can see as much of the garden as is possible. Somewhat wild and unkempt. To one side a little collection of garden furniture – a bench, table, two chairs – forms another seating area.

Two women saunter on stage. They are **Tania** *and* **Varia**. **Tania** *is a blowsy beauty in her thirties, naturally languid and earth-motherly.* **Varia** *is her best friend, slightly older, thinner, darker. A sterner, shrewder presence with a sense of some old unhappiness about her. Varia takes out a cigarette from a silver box and lights it. Varia smokes a lot.*

Varia   The train must be late.

Tania   It's always late

Varia   Why is it always late?

Tania   It always stops at Serpukhov for far too long.

Varia   Yes, I've always wondered why it stops there. I never see anyone get on –

Tania   – Or off, come to that . . . But Sergei won't mind, he likes waiting at stations.

Varia   Kolia won't be happy, though.

They chuckle.

Tania   Mr Punctuality – d'you remember? – always five minutes early, Kolia. At least. I can't wait to see him.

Varia   Me too . . . Maybe we should have gone to the station –

Tania   – Do you think he'll be offended?

Varia   – To make more of a welcome party . . . Perhaps we should've . . . It's been so long.

Tania   I don't know . . . I think Sergei and Natasha will do . . . as a welcome party . . . Don't you? Sergei on his own is enough. Shouts and bear hugs and any excuse for a drink . . . In fact I'm rather glad we're not there . . . We can meet him here, on our own terms, in our own way – not have Sergei as master of ceremonies.

Varia   Yes, yes . . . I just rather wanted to see Kolia step off the train, you know, and look around . . . See him step off the train . . . You know that moment when you're looking at someone and they don't know you've spotted them – just for a second or two they look different, more vulnerable . . . Before they put on their best face and their best manners . . .

This idea is clearly intensely appealing to her. **Tania** *doesn't quite pick up the subtext.*

Tania   I know exactly what you mean . . . And Kolia will be thinking –

Varia   – "Are they here? Where are they?"

Tania   – "Oh my god! Will I recognise them? . . ."

They chuckle together again.

Varia   Oh, he'll recognise Sergei.

Instantly. Sergei hasn't changed.

Tania   He's fatter.

Varia   No, he's always been . . . you know, burly.

Tania   You're too kind to my husband, my dear. He's grown twice the size since Kolia left . . . But he *won't* recognise Natasha . . . She was a girl, a little girl, when Kolia saw her last.

Varia   Of course . . . I suppose you're right. She adored Kolia . . .

Tania   Everybody adores Kolia. We all adore Kolia . . .

Varia   Why aren't we meeting him at the house?

Tania   Well, because he always used to stay here, in the summer house. He loved this summer house, it was his place – just a little distant from the rest of us . . . And the big house isn't the same anymore. Half the rooms empty, dust sheets, the scaffolding . . . No, I wanted to meet him again here. Let him stay here in the summer house – as if nothing had changed.

Varia   "As if" . . .

Tania   Well, we can pretend, for an hour or two.

Varia   Of course we can . . .

They pause. Each thinking about **Kolia** *in their own way.*

Tania   I'm so glad you're here.

Varia   It's a happy accident. "Happy" that there wasn't any cholera in Serpukhov. At least.

Tania   "Cholera", "Cholera" – how I hate that word. I don't know how you can bear it.

Varia   I'm a doctor, I have to –

Tania   – Of course. I know that . . . Still, I can't quite imagine even touching people with cholera. Being close . . .

Varia   Cholera's the least of it, my dear. If you could see some of the –

Tania (*stopping her ears*)   – No, no, don't tell me. I don't want to hear anything horrid.

Varia *says no more.* **Tania** *smiles.*

Tania   We must only think happy thoughts today. Kolia's coming. And to think you're here. You and Kolia meeting again . . . (*Knowingly.*) He'll be surprised. And pleased. I think he'll be moved, in fact.

Varia (*ignoring this*)   Well, I can't stay for long.

Tania   Just a few days. You must promise: I won't be able to cope if you're not here.

Varia   I promise I'll stay as long as I can. After all, they did send me to a cholera epidemic. Even if it didn't happen. I might have been gone months for all they –

Tania   – I can't wait to see him . . .

Varia (*beat*)   Neither can I.

Tania   – Here, on the veranda . . . You know, I think . . . I think Kolia is going to solve all our problems.

Varia   One step at a time, darling – he doesn't have a clue about anything, yet. He thinks he's just coming to stay for a few days, a holiday, see his old friends . . . (*Pause.*) When you wrote you didn't say anything –

Tania   – Not a thing. Not the merest hint . . . No, he suspects nothing, I'm absolutely sure of it – I was all gaiety and fond nostalgia, you'd have been proud of me – not the merest notion of our problems . . . But once he's here and he sees what's happening . . . He has that lawyer's brain, you know, that Moscow lawyer's brain . . . He's so clever, Kolia. He'll see a way through.

Varia   I think we should let him get settled in, first.

Tania   Oh yes, of course. We have to pick our moment very carefully.

Sound of horses' hooves, carriage wheels. They halt.

The two women leap up – their excitement is huge, palpable.

Varia   Here he is!

Tania   Here they are! Not so late after all. How wonderful
. . . I think I'm going to cry.

Varia   No you mustn't! We must be calm. We mustn't show
ridiculous emotion. It'll frighten him – you know Kolia.

On to the stage come **Two Men** *carrying a ladder.*

Tania *and* **Varia**'s *disappointment is as huge and palpable as their
excitement was.*

*The two men wear smocks and clogs. Their rough work clothes are
spattered with paint. One is an older, weatherbeaten man in his 50s
called* **Radish**. *The other is a young man, attractive, with an open
face, called* **Misail**. **Radish** *talks with a regional accent.* **Misail**,
surprisingly, speaks in the same educated tones as **Tania** *and* **Varia**.

Tania   Who are you?

Radish   What?

Varia   What're you doing here?

Radish   What does it look like?

Tania   Go away, we're expecting visitors.

Misail   We've been sent to paint the roof, Ma'am.

The two women subliminally note his accent.

Tania   Who sent you? My husband?

Misail   No –

Radish   – Who's your husband, when he's at home?

Tania   Sergei Sergeivitch Losev.

Radish   Well he didn't send us, whoever he is.

Misail   We were sent by Mr Dolzhikov.

This name has a noticeable effect on the two women.

Tania   Oh . . . Mr Dolzhikov.

Misail Yes. He told us to fix the roof of the summer house.

Varia Dolzhikov sent you . . .

Tania Well, in that case, I suppose you'd better get on with it.

Radish *and* **Misail** *set the ladder up against the summer house.*

Radish Thank you kindly, Madame.

Tania And try not to make too much noise. We're expecting a guest.

Misail You won't even notice us, I promise.

Radish Here, Misail, get the paint.

Misail *exits. The three contemplate each other.*

Tania Why does Mr Dolzhikov want the summer house roof painted?

Radish He didn't confide in me. He said, Radish: paint the roof, then tidy up that summer house. I want it to look just like new.

Varia For what possible reason?

Radish Your guess is as good as mine, Madame. But that's what we're being paid to do.

Misail *comes back with buckets of paint and brushes, sets them down, leaves again.* **Radish** *checks the quality of the paint. It's clear he is always quietly eavesdropping.*

Tania It's too unkind, I think I'm going to cry.

Varia Don't cry, darling. Dolzhikov couldn't have known Kolia was coming.

Tania But it just spoils everything! Workmen on the roof . . .

Varia Kolia won't mind. He'll just be happy to see us.

Misail *comes back in with more paint.*

Varia   Excuse me. What's your name?

Misail   Misail.

Varia   Do you work for Mr Dolzhikov?

Misail   No. For Mr Radish, here.

Varia   So you don't know why Mr Dolzhikov's decided to repaint the summer house either.

Misail   No. I'm afraid not.

Radish (*climbing the ladder*)   Misail!

Misail   Excuse me.

He heads off and begins to climb the ladder with a bucket of paint.

The two women watch the men establish themselves on the roof. They listen in to the conversation.

Radish   Why were you so late this morning?

Misail   I had to go and see the Governor.

Radish   The Governor? Of the province?

Misail   Yes, my father had written to him, to complain.

Radish   About what?

Misail   About the fact that my father doesn't like me doing this job.

Radish   What in god's name has that got to do with the Governor?

Misail   He said that being a housepainter was not consistent with my rank. He said I was not allowed to be a working man. "Not allowed" – can you credit it? It's astonishing. What kind of world do we live in, Radish?

Radish   A very peculiar one, that's for sure.

Misail (*getting angrier*)   This man, this pompous satrap, this . . . popinjay, ordered me to cease working for you – forthwith.

Radish   Well I never –

Misail   – I told him. I said: "Your excellency, please allow me to live my life quietly, causing no offence to anyone, forgotten."

Radish   I bet he didn't like that.

Misail   No. He said I was a "corrupting influence" – can you believe it, Radish? Me: a corrupting influence. He said: what if everyone did exactly as they pleased, paid no heed to their station in life? There would be chaos, revolution, he said. He threatened me.

Radish   Threatened you with what? With a nobleman's life of idleness?

Misail   With "extreme measures". I, of course, refused to change my life.

Radish   You said: "With great respect, your excellency, I refuse to change my life".

Misail (*taken aback*)   Yes . . . Exactly those words. How could you know?

Radish   Oooh . . . I just guessed. Come on, let's get to work.

Misail   There was one thing he asked me – very odd. As I was leaving his office. I was just going out of the door when he called me back. Guess what he asked me?

Radish   "How many virgins are there in Dubechnia?"

Misail   No . . . No. He said: "Are you a vegetarian?"

Radish (*beat*)   Really . . . And what did you reply?

Misail   I said: No, sir, I eat meat.

Radish   Excellent response – come on, get that paint over here.

Down below **Tania** *and* **Varia** *have wandered further out into the garden to watch the men painting.*

Tania   It's so typical of Sergei not to have told me. Typical.

Varia   Do you think he knew?

Tania   Of course he knew. Dolzhikov doesn't own the place
. . . Yet. He can't just come and order buildings repainted
without Sergei's permission . . . And that it should happen
now when Kolia's about to arrive! It's so unfair!

Varia   There are some men on the roof repainting the tiles.
Who's even going to notice?

A serving maid, **Olga***, appears.*

Olga   The tea's brewed Ma'am, shall I bring the samovar?

Tania   No, no, not yet. Wait until they come.

Sound of horses' hooves. A man shouting.

Sergei (*off stage*)   Nous voila! Nous sommes ici!

The women's excitement returns.

Radish *and* **Misail** *are intrigued.*

Tania   Here he is!

Varia (*hiding her emotion*)   At last . . . At last . . .

Tania   Get the tea, Olga, fast as you can!

Olga   Right away, Ma'am.

Olga *dashes off.*

On to the stage strides **A Man***. He's tall, good looking, soberly
dressed in a dark suit. The women turn to him. It's* **Kolia***.*

Kolia   I can't believe it. Here I am.

Varia   And here *we* are. The "vengeful harpies".

The two women run to him. **Tania** *kisses him.*

Tania   Kolia – here at last.

Varia   Little Kolia . . .

She takes his arm, kisses him on the cheek. She holds herself there, just for a second, then her jocular mood returns.

Kolia (*stepping back*)   Look at you all. It's amazing. All these beautiful women. How can you stand it, Sergei? These vengeful harpies fluttering around you day and night?

*He looks round as another man comes on stage carrying **Kolia**'s leather grip. A burly man in slightly flamboyant country clothes – **Sergei**, **Tania**'s husband. He's followed by a young woman, pretty. She takes her bonnet off and checks her hair. This is **Natasha**, **Tania**'s young sister.*

Sergei   You've put on weight, Kolia. All those fancy Moscow restaurants.

He goes into the summer house to put the grip away.

Olga *brings on the samovar and starts arranging the tea things on a side table.* **Natasha** *goes to help her.*

Tania   Nonsense. He hasn't changed at all.

Kolia   I agree. I'm unchanging – it's in my nature. Have I changed, Natasha?

Natasha   Not one iota.

Kolia   But my god, you have. Look at her. She used to be a grubby little minx.

Natasha   Kolia!

Kolia *goes over to* **Tania**, *kisses her forehead.*

Kolia   I'm so happy to be here, I can't believe it.

He looks round as **Sergei** *strides out of the summer house. Steps into the garden to look at the two men on the roof.*

Sergei   Let me know if any tiles need replacing. I don't want you slapping paint on rotten tiles and hoping I won't notice.

Radish   Yes, sir.

Sergei   Don't think you can get away with it either, because I'll be up there daily, checking on you.

Radish   Yes, sir.

Tania   Leave them alone, Sergei. We're trying to pretend they're not there. How can we do that if you're shouting instructions every two minutes?

Sergei (*returning to veranda*)   You've got to let these people know who's boss.

They'll rob you blind otherwise. Have we got any cake?

Tania   Yes, we have cake. Of course we have cake –

Sergei   – If we have cake we must have Madeira –

Tania   – No. No Madeira.

Sergei   Kolia's here, for heaven's sake. We must kill the fatted calf.

Tania (*pointing at dormer*)   Kolia, you're in your usual room.

Kolia   What bliss – you think of everything. To be back in the summer house – marvellous.

Natasha   Kolia here – in the summer house. It doesn't seem real . . .

Sergei (*to* **Olga**)   Olga, bring a bottle of Madeira – no, bring two.

Olga   Right away, sir. (*Leaving.*)

Sergei   Bring two!

Kolia   This is exactly what I needed. I feel ten years younger already . . . It's uncanny, your letter coming like that. I was going berserk – I had to get away. I thought: where can I go? – if I don't have some peace and quiet, they'll have to lock me away. And then your letter came . . .

Tania (*glancing at* **Varia**)   Telepathy . . . You see, it works. No, Varia and I were talking.

We were reading a newspaper and it said, "eminent Moscow lawyer N.V. Podgorin" –

Varia   – "N.V. Podgorin"? I said. Can that be our Kolia? That sounds far too grand and important to be our Mr Punctuality –

Natasha   – Who we used to throw in the river once a week.

Kolia   Yes, you were very cruel, I haven't forgotten, I warn you.

Sergei   Women can be very cruel, yes, indeed . . . Where's that Madeira? Olga!

Kolia   Only Natasha was my friend. Protecting me from you two harpies.

They all laugh. **Kolia** *is very at ease: they are clearly the oldest of friends.*

Tania   How we've missed you. Haven't we missed him, Varia?

Varia   We've thought about you – from time to time, every six months or so . . . Pitying you in Moscow. Even Natasha pities you.

Natasha   I do not! I envy him.

Tania *pushes him over and sits beside him, takes his hand.*

Tania   I'm so happy to see you, Kolia, and you've hardly aged at all. You don't look a day over sixty.

Varia   Sixty-five.

Varia *sits on his other side. Takes his other hand. We may sense how she relishes this physical contact.*

Kolia (*standing up*)   Ha-ha-ha. Natasha, save me from these evil women.

Tania   And you're going to help us, I know it –

Varia (*changing subject quickly*)   – When we saw your name in the newspaper we thought: we have to write to him –

Tania   – And I said: oh, he's bound to have forgotten us.
But we must try and save him –

Varia   – from his eminent legal career. So we wrote you
the letter.

Sergei   I had nothing to do with it, I just want you to know
that. Nothing to do with me. Absolument rien.

Natasha   And they never told me, until the day before
yesterday. Can you imagine?

Tania   We didn't want you to die of excitement, my dear.

Natasha   I was *so* cross. I would have bought a new dress.
Look at me. A country bumpkin.

Kolia   But I love country bumpkins. That's why I'm so fond
of Varia.

He blows a kiss at her. She fends it off.

Varia   Very droll. And none of your insincere kisses,
thank you.

Tania   Who's going to have tea and some delicious
seed cake?

Sergei   Where's that Madeira? Olga!

Varia   So what do you think of the place?

Kolia   Wonderful. Nothing has changed. Exactly as it was
when I left it.

Varia   We call it the Kolia museum. From time to time we
go in there, light a candle and think sorrowfully about you
suffering in Moscow.

Kolia   Most kind.

Tea and cake is served as all this banter is going on.

Radish (*from up above*)   Excuse me?

Sergei *steps off the veranda.*

Sergei   What is it? Can't you see we're entertaining a guest?

Radish   I would say, with great respect, that one in three of these tiles needs to be replaced.

Sergei   Well, replace them.

Radish   We're painters not tilers.

Sergei   Well, leave them unpainted and we'll replace them later.

Radish   That's not going to look very nice, is it? Unpainted tiles all over a freshly painted roof.

Sergei   Well, just paint them, then. I'll replace them later. (*Goes back to veranda.*) Really, these people will rob you blind if you look away for a second.

Kolia   Why're you painting the summer house?

Tania   Yes, why are we painting the summer house?

Sergei   I was, ah, talking it over with Dolzhikov, last time he was up. We were taking a stroll around the park. He said he thought the summer house could do with a lick of paint. I agreed.

Tania   We're not paying for it, are we?

Sergei   No, no. Heaven forfend. Dolzhikov's paying for it.

Tania   But why?

Sergei (*changing subject*)   Kolia, have you seen anything of Vladimir Tomasovitch lately?

Kolia   Not since he died.

Sergei   Has he died? Good god! Shows you how long I've been away from Moscow. Old Vladimir dead? Mon Dieu . . . Gives me quite a turn, that . . . Ah, there you are, Olga. We're dying of thirst here.

Olga *arrives with a bottle of Madeira and some glasses on a tray.*
Sergei *takes it from her.*

Sergei   Now, you can't have seed cake without Madeira.

Olga   I could only find one bottle, sir.

Sergei   Never mind, never mind.

He pours a couple of large glasses.

Sergei   Kolia, here you are.

Kolia   Not for me, old chap.

Sergei   Ladies?

Varia   I'll keep you company.

Tania *shoots her a look: "Traitor".*

Sergei *hands her a glass. Turns away, drains his, refills it covertly, as the others talk.*

Natasha *and* **Kolia** *eye each other up. He's obviously very struck by her.*

Kolia   Look at little Natasha. I can't get over it: the model of a young lady.

Natasha   Young provincial lady. My shabby clothes and my head full of nonsense from all the magazines I read –

Sergei (*snaps fingers*)   – And what's wrong with the provinces? Jamais de ma vie!

(*Snaps fingers.*) Jamais de ma vie!

Kolia *laughs at him.* **Nadia** *joins in.*

Kolia   Look at him – *he* hasn't changed!

Everyone laughs at **Sergei**. *He doesn't mind – he has his Madeira.*

During this **Misail** *has come down the ladder, and busies himself with the paint pots. He spots* **Natasha**, *is instantly taken with her.*

Sergei   Hey, you! Don't I know you?

Misail (*turning*)   I don't think so, sir.

Sergei   Well, I tell you something: you're the very image of the son of Poloznev, the town architect.

Misail   I *am* his son, sir.

Sergei   Oh . . . That would explain it then . . . Right (*Turns.*) Quelle surprise. The architect's son painting the summer house roof. What's happening to the world?

Misail *leaves.* **Natasha** *watches him go, thinking.*

Natasha   Misail Poloznev? . . . How strange.

Varia   Maybe there's a family feud . . . I thought he was oddly well-spoken for a painter.

Kolia   I want to see the house. I want to see the little girls. I want to see everything. The river. The mill pond. The mill.

Varia   Yes, let's all go for a walk.

Kolia   Come along, little Natasha. (*Offering arm.*)

Sergei   Yes, you run along. I'm meeting Dolzhikov here.

He checks his watch.

Tania   Dolzhikov? Here?

Sergei   We've got a couple of things to discuss. I'll see you at supper.

They wander off chatting to themselves.

Olga *comes in, clears away the tea things. Lugs away the samovar.* **Sergei** *doesn't let her take away the Madeira.*

Meanwhile **Sergei** *tops himself up with Madeira. Empties the glass. Refills it, drinks again.*

Man's Voice   Losev? Where are you?

Sergei   Here – by the summer house.

A florid-faced, vulgar and rough-looking man in his 60s comes on to the stage. This is **Dolzhikov**, *the railway engineer. His clothes are garish but conspicuously fine. He has a provincial accent.*

He and **Sergei** *shake hands.* **Sergei** *switches on the charm.*

Sergei Dolzhikov, my dear fellow, lovely to see you.

Dolzhikov Is it open?

Sergei Yes, help yourself. Have a look.

Dolzhikov *goes inside.*

Sergei *empties the Madeira bottle into two glasses.* **Radish** *comes down the ladder, glances at him.* **Sergei** *is pretty stewed by now but disguises it well.* **Radish** *occupies himself with stacking away his paint pots and buckets, covertly listening in. No sign of* **Misail**.

Dolzhikov *comes out.*

Dolzhikov Well, there's a fair amount of room inside. Bigger than I expected. We can lay out the food in there and have room for a band if anyone wants to dance.

Sergei You have to dance at a betrothal party. Oh yes, yes. Il faut dancer, monsieur.

Dolzhikov I speak French.

Sergei Of course, I never –

Dolzhikov – Just because I used to be a grease monkey on the railway doesn't mean I can't speak French, mon-sewer.

Sergei Not in the least surprised, my dear fellow.

Dolzhikov *takes some notes out of his wallet and hands them over.* **Sergei** *pockets them in a flash.*

Dolzhikov There you go . . . (*Looks back at summer house.*) It'll do, I suppose. Get some bunting, some nice coloured lights.

Sergei And who, may I ask, is your daughter betrothed to?

Dolzhikov To the son of the town architect.

Sergei Not? . . . (*Gestures at roof.*) Really?

Dolzhikov He's a strange young chap. Wants to work with his hands, he says, wants to labour like the common man. I said he must be mad – and I should know: I was a grease-monkey on the Belgian railroad. But my Kleopatra won't have anyone else. Claims he's the most interesting man in Dubechnia.

Sergei   As long as they're happy.

Dolzhikov   If you must marry, marry young, I say.

Sergei   I married young . . . You're right. Grow up together, that's the way.

Dolzhikov   D'you know the happiest day of my life? I didn't realise it then but I do now.

Sergei   What?

Dolzhikov   When my dear wife died . . . She died giving birth to our daughter, Kleopatra.

(*He crosses himself.*) God rest her soul. She did me the biggest favour, blessed woman.

Sergei   Really?

Dolzhikov   If she hadn't died I wouldn't be the man I am today . . . Wonderful woman.

Radish *wanders back, readjusts the ladder, makes as if to climb up.*

Dolzhikov   Radish! Where's that Misail?

Radish   We've run out of sandpaper, he's gone into town to get some more.

Dolzhikov   Well, make sure you do a proper job.

Radish   Of course, sir. We aim to please.

Dolzhikov   And you can tell that Misail that my daughter, Miss Kleopatra, is coming up with a picnic for him.

Radish   I shall pass that information on, sir.

He begins to climb. **Misail** *enters, roll of sandpaper in hand – sees* **Dolzhikov** *and recoils. Hides himself round the side of the house.*

Dolzhikov (*turning to* **Sergei**)   What about music. D'you know a good little orchestra?

Sergei   Yes, I could certainly arrange it. Be very happy to
. . . They're a little pricey, though – They'll want money up
front, also . . .

He and **Dolzhikov** *wander off chatting,* **Dolzhikov** *handing him
some more notes.*

Misail *emerges, looks round cautiously, then climbs up the ladder.*

Radish   You just missed your prospective father-in-law.

Misail   Oh, really? What did he want?

Radish   You're having your betrothal party here, in case
you didn't know.

Misail   Aw, no . . . No, please . . . I don't want a party. It
must be Kleopatra's idea.

Radish   Oh yes, and Miss Kleopatra's coming up here with
a picnic for you.

Misail   For god's sake! What working man has a picnic
brought to him by his fiancée? It's preposterous. No matter
what I do they try to spoil it. They try to undermine me at
every turn . . .

He starts sanding away in a fury.

Radish   Well, forgive me for saying this but you're hardly a
typical working man: son of the town architect, getting
married to the daughter of a millionaire . . . Come off it,
Misail.

Misail   It doesn't make any difference. I work with my
hands, I'm an ordinary painter, like you – I'm no different
from millions of other working men.

Radish *lets him reflect on this fantasy.*

Down below **Natasha** *appears.* **Misail** *spots her and is immediately
taken again – fascinated. We can see he's somewhat smitten. He
covertly watches her go into the summer house looking for* **Kolia**,
knocking on the door gently.

Radish *is oblivious, carries on painting and talking.*

Radish   What do you really want to do? Sail away on an ocean clipper? Join the cavalry? Become a priest?

Misail   I long for a simple life. That's why I want to work with my hands. It's very straightforward: I want to do a fair day's work for a fair day's wage.

Radish *looks at him, curious.*

Radish   Why do you want to work with your hands? It's hard, you know. Unforgiving –

Misail   – Yes. Yes, and that's good. Life is hard and unforgiving. So it's good that work is hard and unforgiving because everybody should know about the struggle for existence and what it's really like. Why should the strong enslave the weak? Why should the minority – the rich and powerful – draw the living sap out of the majority. Everyone should work with their hands, then they'd understand what life was really like.

Radish   Life . . . So what is life like? Eh?

Misail   I'm, well . . . It should be, I don't know . . . Life should be . . . above all . . . honourable.

Radish *laughs sardonically.*

Radish   You're priceless, Misail. "Life should be honourable" – I love that . . .

Misail   So: you tell me, then. What *is* life like?

Radish   "What is life like"? It's as if you asked me: what's a carrot like? A carrot is a carrot and nothing more . . . That's all there is to it.

He turns round and starts painting.

Natasha *comes out of the summer house, looks up.* **Misail** *gives her a big smile.*

Misail   Can I help you, miss?

Natasha   Ah, no, I was just looking for someone. Doesn't matter. Thank you.

Misail   You're most welcome.

She saunters off. **Misail** *watches her go. Turns back to his painting.*

Down below, **Tania**, **Varia** *and* **Kolia** *come on stage back from their walk. The mood is serious.*

Kolia   – You're saying he's spent *everything*? All the money?

Tania   Everything. All on his crazy schemes. We're ruined.

Varia   Would you like to see eight half-built summer cottages?

Kolia   But when I lived here you were well off – I mean not rolling in money, but there was nothing to worry about, financially –

Tania   – That was my legacy from my father: or rather mine and Natasha's. The capital's long gone. Now all we have is the estate. I don't know how many mortgages Sergei's taken out on the land. He refuses to tell me.

Kolia   He means well, Sergei, he's full of ideas –

Tania   – Darling, you know he has ten new ideas every day. The tannery –

Varia   – And the spa. And the pedigree cattle herd. Oh, and he was going to bribe the railway engineer to move the station ten miles closer to us. Can you imagine? At least we managed to stop that one.

Kolia   But there was a lot of money – you were rich, Tania.

Varia   She *was* rich. Then she married Sergei . . .

Tania (*keeping tears back*)   The mortgages are due in a week. The banks will foreclose on the loans. Everything's going to be sold. The house, the estate . . .

She reaches for **Varia** *and they hug each other.*

Varia   You have to help us, Kolia. You're our only hope.

Kolia   Me? . . . Of course, of course, whatever I can. But, I'm a lawyer, not a businessman.

Tania   You have a lawyer's brain. You'll see a way out of all this.

Varia   We just need someone who Sergei trusts. He won't listen to us any more.

Kolia *is becoming progressively more unhappy. They move to the bench and chairs.*

Tania   I'll show you all the papers, the bank loans, the deeds, the mortgages . . . My head reels when I look at them. We all thought – when we realised everything was almost lost –

Varia   – We thought: Kolia. We need Kolia to sort out this mess.

Tania   And I tell you, Kolia, when I heard you were coming. I felt happy, for the first time in months. I woke with a smile on my face . . .

Tania *takes* **Kolia**'s *hand, smiles at him.* **Varia** *lights a cigarette.*

Tania   We'll fetch them now. They're all in Sergei's study. Come on, Varia, help me. Not a moment to lose.

Varia   You see, I knew he'd come to our rescue.

They leave. **Kolia** *stands there – perplexed, troubled. He goes slowly into the summer house.*

The lights change.

Scene Two

It's morning. Bright and fresh. Birdsong.

Kolia *comes out onto the veranda with files and documents in his hands and dumps them on the table.* **Sergei** *follows, a coffee cup in hand.* **Kolia** *checks some of the papers.* **Sergei** *turns his back to*

Kolia *and takes a hip flask out of his pocket. He adds some liquor to his coffee.*

Radish *is sitting on the roof. Not painting, but listening impassively. The ladder is still there.*

Kolia   My god . . . I see what you mean . . . What a mess . . .

Sergei   Well, you've seen everything. I've held nothing back, I swear. You now have the full, ghastly nightmare laid out before you . . .

Kolia   I just don't understand these investments you made . . . In Japan, of all places. Thousands of roubles. Why Japan? What do you know of Japan?

Sergei   Well, I met this Japanese businessman. He spoke excellent French, by the way. The Orient was about to open her arms to the West, he said. He assured me I'd make a killing – a complete killing. It seemed a perfect opportunity . . . Do you want to walk out with a gun, before lunch, see if we can pot something?

Kolia   No.

Sergei   Fine . . .

Kolia   Where did you meet this Japanese businessman?

Sergei   In a brothel, I'm ashamed to say. Do you remember that time you and I went to that place on Zhivordiorka street? What was that little girl I had called? Armenian, I think. Fifteen, sixteen?

Kolia   I can't remember. But you also seem to have accepted the most ruinous rates of interest. There was no need to repay on these terms –

Sergei (*snaps his fingers*)   – "Before he said 'Alas, alack' a bear had sat upon his back" –

Kolia　– Sergei: concentrate. We have to go to the bank and renegotiate the interest. It's daylight robbery. That's the first thing –

Sergei　– Elle etait tres mignonne, la petite Armenienne . . . What about a hare? Hundreds of hares in the big wood. We could bag a couple in five minutes.

Distant bell ringing.

Sergei　Too late. I'm needed at the house.

Kolia *closes the files.*

Kolia　How much time have we got?

Sergei　Just under a week.

Kolia *looks at him, as if to say "forget it".*

Sergei *goes down the steps.*

Sergei　"The Orient is opening her arms to the West". Those were his very words. It was irresistible, Kolia – he said I couldn't lose, guaranteed twenty five percent return on the capital investment in the first year . . .

He turns and wanders off. **Radish** *climbs down the ladder. Glances at* **Kolia** *immersed in the papers and leaves the stage.*

Natasha (*off*)　Kolia? Are you there? Are you awake?

Kolia　Yes, yes. Come and join me.

Quickly he gathers up the papers, folds the files closed. Pushes them to one side. **Natasha** *appears. She's wearing a straw hat and a white floaty dress. She looks very beautiful.*

She kisses him good morning and sits down beside him.

Kolia　You look ravishing.

Natasha　I thought I might wear this to the betrothal party, with a sash and a different hat, of course.

Kolia　What betrothal party?

Natasha   Dolzhikov's daughter and the architect's son.
Sergei has rented them the summer house – for some
dubious reason. I think he thinks Dolzhikov might be good
for a loan. Anyway, there'll be an orchestra. We're all invited.
You must stay: we'll all go – do say yes – it'll be fun.

Kolia   It's nothing to do with me.

Natasha   Of course it is. If you say you want to go, then
Tania and Varia will come as well.

Kolia   All right – possibly. Do you want some coffee?

Natasha   I'll have a sip of yours.

She takes his cup and has a sip, replaces it.

Kolia   What do we do at this betrothal party? Look at the
locals and laugh behind our hands?

Natasha   Yes . . . But we can also dance, ourselves.

Kolia   Oh, dancing, I forgot.

Natasha   Maybe we could have a dance, Kolia, you and me.
I remember when I was little you used to dance with me.

Kolia   Did I?

Natasha   Yes, I used to stand on your shoes and you
showed me how to waltz.

Kolia   Did I really? I think I've forgotten how to dance.

Natasha   Don't be silly – no one forgets how to dance.
Stand up.

She takes his hand and raises him to his feet.

Natasha   Now, pretend it's a waltz.

*She holds out her hands and **Kolia** takes her in his arms. **Natasha**
hums a simple waltz tune and they begin to waltz around.*

Natasha   There, you see. You hadn't forgotten at all.

Kolia *is enjoying the sensation of having this young girl in his arms.*

Kolia   Yes, I think I'm getting the hang of it. Slowly but surely . . . Keep going . . .

They dance on. Unobserved by them, **Tania** *and* **Varia** *have crept round the side of the summer house and are looking on with much pleasure.*

Then **Radish** *and* **Misail** *return with fresh pails of paint and their brushes.* **Kolia** *sees them and stops abruptly.*

Radish   Don't mind me, sir. Very pretty picture.

Kolia   Morning.

Misail (*big smile*)   Good morning.

Natasha   Good morning.

Kolia *and* **Natasha** *separate.* **Radish** *dumps the pails and* **Misail** *climbs up onto the roof.*

Tania *and* **Varia** *reveal themselves.*

Tania   Well, good morning. Practising for the betrothal party?

Kisses are exchanged.

Kolia   It's all a bit much for me. I'm quite out of breath.

Varia   Poor old fellow. You've tired him out, Natasha. Look at him wheezing.

Kolia   Who wants some coffee?

Tania   We have to go into town. Come along Natasha, the carriage is waiting. Goodbye everyone.

Varia   I'll join you, old man.

Kolia   See you later.

Kolia *goes into the summer house for another cup.* **Tania** *and* **Natasha** *leave.* **Varia** *looks up at* **Misail** *on the roof.* **Radish** *is checking the paint.*

Varia   Good morning!

Misail   Good morning, Madame.

Radish   Good morning to you, Ma'am. Lovely day.

Radish *leaves.*

Kolia *comes out with a cup and goes to the coffee pot and pours a cup for* **Varia**. *She sits down and takes out a cigarette.* **Kolia** *takes off his jacket.*

Varia   I recognise that man from somewhere, the older man . . . You look quite flushed. Is that exercise . . . or Natasha?

Kolia   Ha-ha. Though I must say she's very beautiful.

Varia   Oh, she's incredibly beautiful. All the young men want to marry her.

Kolia   Really? I hope she finds somebody . . . nice.

Varia   Nice . . . And rich, would be handy. Any news?

They're very relaxed together. From the way she glances at him when he's not looking it's clear she had once been in love with him – her gaze is full of unrequited longing but her dry ironic tone never falters.

Kolia   I've been through the papers and . . .

Varia   And? –

Kolia   – Hopeless. The loans are all completely valid. He knew exactly what he was doing . . . I think we're stumped. Unless we can borrow some money somewhere . . .

Varia   Can't we have him declared insane?

They both laugh at this, then their laughs die. They sit there thinking for a moment.

Kolia   He's going to have to find some money – fast. If only to buy some time.

Varia   Why aren't you married, Kolia?

Kolia *(a bit taken aback)*   What? Me? . . . Why aren't *you*?

Varia   I'm a dried out old doctor who works in a factory hospital and smokes too much. Who'd have me?

Kolia   Lots of men.

Varia   Then where are they? But, *you've* no excuse. Good looking, successful, a "Moscow lawyer"! You must be fighting the women off.

Kolia   Well – It's . . . (*Pauses.*) I don't know . . . I can talk to you, Varia . . . How wonderful it is to talk to an old friend. The truth is that, from time to time, I do meet someone, and I think – "Perhaps this is the one?" . . . But somehow nothing seems to come of it.

Varia *looks at him – for a moment we see the old longing again – then it's gone. She braces herself: this is still hard.*

Varia   May I be honest with you, Kolia?

Kolia   Oh dear. I expect nothing else from you. Fire away.

Varia (*pause*)   You should marry Natasha.

Kolia   What? Natasha? . . . Come on, Varia, be reasonable . . . She's just a child. A beautiful child, yes, but still –

Varia   – Not any more. She's a beautiful young woman. And she loves you: we can all see it . . . Tania and I were talking about it this morning.

Kolia   Well you can stop talking about it. I can't think of Natasha in that way –

Varia   – Nonsense. Remember who you're talking to. Seriously, you should consider it.

Kolia   I'm not ready to be married. I think that's my problem . . . Not even to Natasha –

Varia   – No: your problem is that you can't see happiness when it's standing there in front of you. You can't imagine being happy with someone . . . Like Natasha. Don't run away from happiness, Kolia. You should take it – especially when it's offered to you on a plate . . .

Kolia *thinks. Gets up, walks around.*

Kolia   "Happiness" . . . Why does everyone talk about "happiness"? What does it mean? After happiness comes unhappiness . . . After youth comes old age. Nobody can be healthy and cheerful all their lives. You have to be ready for anything. You have to work, you have to endure . . . You do your duty as best as you can . . .

Varia   That's a bit harsh, isn't it? A bit bleak . . .

Kolia   You're a doctor, you see life as it's really lived. Tell me I'm wrong.

Varia *says nothing. She stands up.*

Kolia (*smiles*)   Anyway, what would Natasha want with an old bachelor like me?

Varia (*taking his arm*)   She'd make you young again.

Kolia   I don't want to be young again. I hated being young. You remember what I was like. I was appalling! Come on, let's go and find Sergei. See if we can talk some sense into him.

They wander off, talking, reminiscing and pass **Radish** *as he comes in with a couple of tins of paint.* **Radish** *glances at them.*

Radish   Lice eat grass. Rust eats iron. Lies eat the soul.

He dumps the paint pots at the foot of the ladder and exits.

Up on the roof **Misail** *watches them go. He turns to his work.*

Girl's Voice   Coo-eee! It's me!

A pretty young woman, with dark hair and conspicuous makeup comes onto the stage with a travelling rug and a picnic basket. She is **Dolzhikov**'s *daughter,* **Kleopatra**, *in her 20s, expensively and flashily dressed.*

Misail   Kleopatra? . . . What's going on?

Kleopatra   Lunch, silly. You've got to eat.

She sets down the basket and flaps out the travelling rug on the grass in front of the veranda, humming to herself, as **Misail** *wearily* *climbs down the ladder. And looks on – hugely frustrated. He looks around. No sign of* **Radish**.

Misail   No, Kleopatra, I told you. No more picnics. Please. How can I claim to be an honest working man if you bring me a lunch like this every day? It's ridiculous. Thank god it's only Radish.

If there were other workers here I'd be a laughing stock.

Kleopatra (*paying no attention*)   It's only a bit of salmon.

Misail (*opening basket*)   A bit of salmon in aspic, with pickled cucumbers. And a plum tart and cold white wine and chocolates. I have my bread and my cheese – it's enough for me.

Kleopatra   Fiddle-de-dee. Sit down. Sit down beside me.

She sits down coquettishly on the rug. With bad grace **Misail** *sits beside her.*

Kleopatra   I like to see you. I miss seeing you – knowing you're up here working. You like to see me too, don't you?

She shuffles closer to him.

Misail   Yes, of course. It's just that . . . It's very nice of you. I'm glad you came.

Kleopatra   "Nice" . . . "Glad" . . . You don't have a passionate vocabulary, Misail. I longed to see you, so I came.

Misail   I'm . . . Delighted. Supremely happy.

Kleopatra (*moving closer*)   Don't you love this estate?

Misail   Yes. It's very handsome – the old house needs some work, though.

Kleopatra   Father told me that the owners are very badly in debt, seriously.

Misail   That's a shame – they seem very nice – very agreeable.

Kleopatra   Father thinks that when the mortgages come due he can buy it for next to nothing.

Misail   Why would he want to do that?

Kleopatra   But it has a spirit, don't you think? Even this old summer house. A great spirit of place. I could be very happy here, living a simple life . . .

Misail   Yes . . .

Kleopatra   With my loved one.

She takes his hands.

Kleopatra   Oh, Misail, Misail, I'm so happy, so excited . . .

Misail   What's going on? Kleopatra –

Kleopatra   – I thank god for you, Misail.

Misail   You do? Why?

Kleopatra   Because you're the most interesting man in this town.

Misail   Am I?

Kleopatra   Without you this town would be nothing. A pimple on the face of Russia.

Misail   Really?

Kleopatra   You're the son of an architect but you said to hell with all this snobbery. "I want to be a simple working man" you said – and, by God, you went and did it. The whole town laughs at you but you don't care. You tell your father to go and fry himself. You don't give a hoot for his old-fashioned values.

Misail   Well, it isn't quite like –

Kleopatra   – You have a pure spirit, an honest heart. You're interesting, fascinating. You break the rules, you tell people to go to hell –

Misail   – I just want to lead my life. Quietly, giving offence to no-one, Forgotten. I want to do an honest day's work for an honest –

Kleopatra   – Exactly! (*She kisses him.*) That's why I always knew you were the one for me. That's why I knew this place would be perfect for us.

Misail   What're you talking about?

Kleopatra   Father is going to buy this estate – for me – when the mortgages come due.

Misail   For you, this whole estate? –

Kleopatra   – Yes! And you and I are going to go and live in the big house and rebuild it and make the farms work again. We'll dam the river and stock it with fish. We'll have a mill, to mill flour. We'll bring in harvests. We'll plant woods. It'll be wonderful, Misail. A real life, it's what I long for: a true, honest life . . .

Misail   Kleopatra, just one second –

Kleopatra   – But I can't do it on my own. I need someone strong with me. A strong independent spirit who cares nothing for convention . . .

She grabs him and they kiss again. She pushes him back onto the rug.

Kleopatra (*whispering*)   I need someone strong, Misail, I need someone strong . . .

She stops. Looks around.

Kleopatra   I've got a better idea.

She stands up, draws **Misail** *to his feet.*

She picks up the rug.

Kleopatra   Take the basket.

Misail (*doing so*)   What's going on? –

Kleopatra (*meaningfully*) – We're going to have our picnic in a very private clearing where nobody can see us. All alone, just you and me, my darling, alone in the woods . . .

She grabs his hand and she leads him swiftly off stage. **Misail** *protesting.*

Misail   No, Kleopatra, really. I really shouldn't leave the summer house . . .

The lights change.

Scene Three

It's late afternoon. **Varia**, **Tania** *and* **Natasha** *enter.*

Tania   I thought he said he'd come to the house.

Varia   I didn't hear a carriage.

Natasha   Maybe he's having a nap.

She goes into the summer house. We hear her voice.

Natasha (*V.O.*)   Kolia? Are you there?

Varia   He would've come to find us.

Tania   Maybe the news is too awful.

Natasha (*coming out*)   No sign. I don't think he's come back.

Tania   He must have gone back to the bank in Serpukhov, then. He said he might – if he had no luck in Dubechnia.

Varia   Well, he's certainly doing his best.

Tania   Yes he is, bless him . . . Even for a doomed cause.

Varia   He's very diligent, Kolia, when he sets his mind to something.

Natasha *sits down. So does* **Tania**. **Varia** *prowls around.*

Tania   Doesn't take no for an answer.

Varia (*dryly*)   Doesn't take "yes" for an answer, either.

Tania   But he works hard.

Natasha   I think he works too hard. He's meant to be here for a rest and we've got him running hither and thither like a farm manager.

Tania   He's happy to do it, darling. He's practically a member of the family. He wants to help.

Natasha   Why doesn't he just – (*She stops.*)

Varia   Just what?

Natasha   – Just relax. Be himself – was he like that as a young man? Always . . . I don't know, making a joke out of things . . . deliberately taking the wrong inference.

Tania   He was very shy as a young man, wouldn't you say, Varia? When we first met him, when he first came to stay here?

Varia   No. Not shy at all.

Tania   I always thought he was over shy.

Natasha   I don't think he's shy. I think he's . . . obtuse.

Tania   That's an interesting word: "obtuse". What exactly does it mean?

Natasha   *You* know what I mean, Varia – you know Kolia better than anyone – that way he has of . . . of missing the point. I think he does it deliberately, sometimes.

Varia   Yes . . .

Tania   I'm completely baffled. What're you talking about, darling?

Natasha   I really like Kolia . . . (*A little embarrassed.*) I think he's kind, he's funny, he's handsome . . . I mean, I want him to look at me as . . . well, not as a "grubby little minx" . . . I mean, what is it about some men?

This is hard for **Varia**. *She lights a cigarette.*

Tania   Oh, don't get on to that subject. Men! Kolia is the
best of men. I could tell you a thing or two about men. Kolia
is a paragon amongst men – wouldn't you say, Varia?

Varia   I don't know about "paragon". He's certainly kind,
funny and handsome. But you don't want to idealise a
person, not even –

Natasha (*frustration breaking out*)   – I mean what does one
have to do? How does one have to behave to get . . .? I don't
know – to get some understanding, some honesty? How do
you show a man, Varia, that you're sincere, that you're not a
silly child any more? That you have feelings . . .

Tania   No, no, no. You do nothing. Men understand that,
instinctively. Sometimes that's the whole problem, believe
you me.

Natasha   Does Kolia understand that? Does he know what
I'm thinking, while we're talking to each other about this
and that? What I'm feeling inside? . . .

(*To* **Varia**.) You know him so well, Varia. Does Kolia know?
Can he tell?

Varia *looks at* **Natasha** *in her anguish. It's almost too much to bear.
She tries to cover things up.*

Varia   I'm not sure. Kolia . . . The thing about Kolia . . .
Sometimes you think: yes. And then . . . (*Memories flooding
in.*) Well, he goes his own way, if you know what I mean. It's
very hard to tell. Once, I remember we – (*She almost tears-up.*)
Goodness, I'm starving . . .

She stands up. **Tania** *realises what's happening.*

Tania   Yes, let's all have some supper. I'm hungry too. Look
at the time. We'll leave a plate for Kolia.

They stand and begin to wander off. **Natasha** *oblivious to* **Varia**'s
mood.

Natasha   But Tania – when Sergei was courting you –

Tania   – I don't think "courting" is the right expression, darling.

She and **Varia** *manage a laugh at this.* **Natasha** *walks ahead, sounding off.* **Tania** *takes* **Varia**'*s hand, squeezes it.*

Natasha   But you weren't in a kind of a maddening limbo . . . a maddening limbo of uncertainty, of ignorance, trying to interpret every gesture –

Tania   – I would just let things take their natural course. All in good time, you know?

They exit, their voices dwindle.

Dolzhikov, **Radish** *and* **Misail** *enter.* **Dolzhikov** *shins up the ladder, has a look at the roof.*

Dolzhikov   You'd better get a bloody move on, you two. I want the whole place smartened up. I want it looking like new.

Radish *climbs up.*

Radish   It's these tiles – they're warped and split. They need to be sanded and filled with putty.

We're going as fast as we can, aren't we, Misail?

Misail   Yes. We're only trying to do a proper job.

Dolzhikov   Just slap some paint on. It's only for one night. It can fall down after that, for all I care. So, shift your arse, Radish.

(*To* **Misail**.) Hold on, sonny, I want a word.

Misail *was about to climb up. He stops and steps back.* **Dolzhikov** *descends the ladder, beckons him to one side.*

Radish   Lice eat grass. Rust eats iron. Lies eat the soul.

Dolzhikov (*looking up*)   What's that?

Radish   We'll go flat out, sir. Don't you worry.

He turns back to his painting. But he's keeping his ears open.
Dolzhikov *draws* **Misail** *aside.*

Dolzhikov   Now. Kleopatra.

Misail (*suddenly worried*)   Yes, sir?

Dolzhikov   What's going on? Don't lie to me – I can see a lie in a man's face at a hundred versts.

Misail   Ah. Right. She came up for a picnic, we went into the woods, then one thing led to another, and –

Dolzhikov   – And did she tell you?

Misail   What?

Dolzhikov   About the estate?

Misail (*disguising his relief*)   Oh . . . She did mention something . . . That you were going to buy it.

Dolzhikov   Well, not a word to anyone. I tried to buy it off them last year. I knew they were in trouble, you see. Offered a fair price but that Sergei Sergeivitch just laughed at me. His mortgages are due in a matter of days: the bailiffs will seize everything – every last hay bale and horseshoe. That's when yours truly steps in and picks it up for a song . . . Think you and Kleopatra can manage it?

Misail   I was really hoping to carry on with Radish for a while longer. I still have a lot to learn . . .

Dolzhikov   My son-in-law can't go around in clogs and a painter's smock! I'm sorry, I just don't understand you, Misail, but once you're betrothed to Kleopatra you're joined to the Dolzhikov family.

It's a whole different world, believe me.

Misail   Right, yes . . . I understand, sir.

Dolzhikov   Anyway: not a word about the estate. They think I'm interested in this summer house – a "first home for my daughter and son-in-law". He's prepared to let it to me at an exorbitant rent. That's all you know. Right, sonny?

Misail   I completely understand.

Dolzhikov *looks at* **Misail**.

Dolzhikov   Cheer up! You're getting betrothed to the richest girl in Dubechnia province. You're not under sentence of death!

Misail   I'm very happy, sir.

Dolzhikov *draws him further aside.*

Dolzhikov   I know my Kleopatra . . . has she been getting fresh? Eh? Inviting you into the hayloft for a tumble? A bit of slap and tickle? Hunt the hamster?

Misail   Certainly not, sir.

Dolzhikov   If she does – just give her a clout. There'll be plenty of time for that when you're married.

Countess or chambermaid: that's one thing all women understand.

Misail   What's that?

Dolzhikov   A slap in the face and a kick in the arse. I used to slap my wife from time to time – god bless her departed soul – and I used to tell her: "You'll thank me for this, my dear, you will thank me one day." . . .

(*He tears-up briefly.*) Wonderful woman . . . She died giving birth to Kleopatra, you know. It was the best thing she ever did for me – made me the man I am today . . . Did I ever tell you that?

Misail   Yes, sir, you did.

Dolzhikov (*pause*)   Hadn't you better get back to work?

He strides off. **Misail** *wearily climbs back up the ladder and picks up his paint brush.* **Radish** *smiles at him.*

They move round to the "back" of the roof to paint there, out of sight.

The light changes.

Scene Four

The afternoon has advanced. Dusk.

Kolia *comes out of the summer house with* **Sergei***'s papers. He spreads them on the table. Sits down, takes out a pen.*

It's all impossible. Wearisome. He makes the odd note from time to time. Then he pushes them aside in exasperation.

Natasha *comes out of the summer house to join him, bringing him a cup of coffee.*

Kolia   Thank you, Natasha: you can read my mind.

Natasha   It's just how you like it: sweet and with a splash of warm milk. I remembered.

Kolia   What would I do without – (*Stops himself.*) I'm sure it's delicious. Thank you.

He has a sip. Makes an appreciative noise.

Natasha   May I ask you something, Kolia?

Kolia   Of course, sit down.

She does so, bringing her chair closer to his. She gestures at the files.

Natasha   What's going to happen?

Kolia   I don't know . . . I think Sergei is going to have to go back to the banks to ask for a little more time.

Natasha   But if he can't get it?

Kolia   Then the loans fall due. And if he can't pay, then, I'm afraid, the banks will seize the estate. It'll belong to them.

Natasha   I was thinking about that, I was thinking that if the estate is sold then Sergei will go away – to work, to find a job somewhere – and our life will change completely. I can't stay with my sister because I'll just be a burden to her and the family. So I shall have to get a job.

Kolia   Of course, if the worst comes to the worst –

Natasha   – I thought I could get a job in Moscow and send money to Tania and Sergei, and the children, wherever they happened to be

Kolia   Yeees . . . What kind of job were you thinking of?

Natasha   I've no idea. You could guide me, though, give me advice.

Kolia   Mmm, well . . . It depends on your qualifications.

Natasha   I have no qualifications. But you could help me, Kolia, couldn't you? Otherwise I don't know what I'll do . . .

She chokes up a bit. **Kolia** *looks into her eyes.*

She's very beautiful and very needy. He squeezes her shoulder.

Kolia   Don't cry, Natasha. It's not worth crying about.

Natasha   But it is! How can you say that? It's everything we have.

Kolia *takes a signet ring off his finger. He hands it to her.*

Kolia   Read what's inside.

Natasha (*reading*)   "All things pass" . . . Why do you have this written on your ring?

Kolia   Because when I'm sad these words make me cheerful . . . And when I'm cheerful and happy, they make me sad . . . "All things pass", life will pass. You need nothing, Natasha. All you need is the feeling of freedom, for when someone is free he – or she – needs nothing. Nothing, nothing.

I'm free, Natasha. You're free: don't waste your tears on this house, on these woods and fields.

All things pass.

Natasha *thinks. She hands the ring back to him.*

Natasha   Is this your philosophy?

Kolia *(fitting ring)*   Yes, I suppose so. It helps me. Helps me get through.

Natasha   Through what?

Kolia   Life.

Pause. **Natasha** *seems suddenly overwhelmed again.*

Natasha   There's one thing missing.

Kolia   What's that?

Natasha *(taking his hand)*   Is there no room for love in your philosophy of life? . . .

This really draws him up short, as if he's never considered it before. But before he can reply, they're interrupted.

Varia *(calling)*   Hello, hello . . .

They look round. **Varia** *and* **Tania** *approach the summer house.*

Tania   I told you we'd find the lovebirds out here. Oh, yes . . .

Varia   Don't let us interrupt your "intimate" conversation –

Tania   – Sweet nothings and all that . . .

The two women laugh. **Kolia** *pretends to ignore the implications.*

Natasha   Don't be silly, you two – Kolia's going to help me get a job in Moscow.

Kolia *extracts his hand from* **Natasha**'s*. He's irritated, uncomfortable at this interpretation of events. He manages to keep his smile going as* **Tania** *and* **Varia** *climb up the steps.*

Tania   Supper's ready. We felt like a stroll so we thought we'd come and fetch you.

Natasha *stands.*

Kolia   Do you know, I think I've got a bit of a headache. Too much reading. I think I might have an early night.

Tania   All right, we'll see you in the morning.

Natasha   Think of a job I could do in Moscow.

Varia   How about "heartbreaker"?

They chuckle and wander off with calls of "good night", "sleep well". **Varia** *drops her shawl and doesn't notice.* **Kolia** *steps off the veranda and goes to pick it up.*

Kolia   Varia!

She turns and comes back. The others go on.

Varia   Thank you, kind sir.

Kolia (*a bit tense*)   There's nothing going on, is there?

Varia   What do you mean?

Kolia   There's no sort of plan. A little scheme you and Tania have hatched between you.

Varia   No.

Kolia   With Natasha . . . You haven't been speaking to her, have you? You and Tania?

Varia   We speak to her all the time.

Kolia   You haven't been putting ideas in her head?

Varia   You're talking in riddles, Kolia, my dear. What are you trying to say?

Kolia   Nothing. Forget it. I'll see you in the morning.

Varia   She loves you very much, you know.

Kolia   Well, she hasn't told me.

Varia   She doesn't need to tell you. It beams out of her eyes every time she catches sight of you.

Kolia   A young girl's infatuation. It's nothing. She'll forget me the second I've gone.

Varia   She'll never forget you, Kolia.

She stares at him, deadly serious. **Kolia** *is shaken, somewhat. This is all getting out of hand.*

She smiles and wanders off. Not looking back.

Varia   Sweet dreams . . .

Kolia *thinks for a moment. Gathers up the papers, goes into the summer house.*

The lights dim.

Scene Five

The lanterns glow. Night falls. The windows of the summer house are lit.

Crickets chirp, an owl hoots.

Sergei *emerges from the darkness. He's drunk. He has a bottle of brandy and two glasses in his hand.*

Sergei   Kolia? Are you there?

Kolia *steps outside in his shirt sleeves. He can't believe it. Tiredly –*

Kolia   Yes. Yes, I'm here.

Sergei   Excusez moi, old chum – Sorry to intrude, but it's the only way we can get a proper drink in this house after supper. Have to make myself scarce. Otherwise Varia and Tania moan on endlessly about alcoholism. Said I was popping over to talk about the bank – seemed to satisfy them.

He sits down and pours two large glasses.

Kolia   Just the one.

Sergei   Oh yes, just the one, mon ami.

They clink glasses. **Sergei** *drains his and tops it up.*

Sergei   I just wanted to say, Kolia, old friend, thanks for all
your help. I know it's a lost cause, but it's at times like these
that old friends, real friends, you know . . . are worth their
weight in gold. Unhappy choice of phrase, that – but are
what make the friendship stand on foundations of . . .
through thick and thin, can be relied on . . . We tried, we
tried to reason with those *bastards* at the bank. But we failed.
But we tried, honourably, as gentlemen, and we failed . . .

He pours himself another drink.

Kolia   If only you'd come to me earlier, Sergei. It's pointless
to say this now: but you left it so late. It was time – time was
our enemy.

Sergei   "Time was our enemy" . . . Who can conquer time?
Nobody . . . Time's winged chariot – there's a phrase for
you. It wouldn't have made any difference. I'm the wrong
sort of person for this modern world. Cut from a different
cloth, don't you know? I'm an idealist . . . I have high ideals
and everyone else has got their snouts in the trough . . .

That's exactly my problem, you see: I'm an idealist in a
world where money is king. If you don't want to end up in
the gutter you have to bow down before the "god" money.
But I won't do it. No, I refuse. I will not contaminate myself
with –

Kolia   – Have they set a date for the auction?

Sergei   Ah, yes, I believe they have . . . Tuesday.

Kolia   Jesus Christ . . . Then there's nothing for it.

Sergei *begins to grow emotional. Pours another drink, downs it.*

Sergei   My dear friend, my old friend. Save me . . . Lend
me two hundred roubles –

Kolia   – What?

Sergei   Just to see me by. I owe someone some money, rather urgently, and he's making all sorts of unreasonable threats. It would be very embarrassing, you know, for Tania, if they –

Kolia *takes out his wallet. Places a few notes on the table. He's angry now.* **Sergei** *sweeps them up, pockets them rapidly.*

Sergei   Thank you, bless you, brother-in-law.

Kolia   What did you say?

Sergei   I'm jumping the gun, but "in name", as it were: brother-in-law-to-be, if you'd rather. Natasha's a lovely girl. Lovely . . . Très jolie. Don't worry, I'll pay you back. It'll be wonderful to have you as a member of the family.

Kolia (*standing up*)   – Just do me one favour, Sergei. Don't ever describe yourself as an "idealist" any more. It makes me sick to my stomach –

Sergei   – Steady on . . . But I *am*. I love freedom, I love –

Kolia (*losing it*)   – You've frittered away your wife's entire fortune!

A considerable one at that! Aren't you ashamed of yourself? . . . Aren't you disgusted living out your life like this? . . . Pointless chatter, affectations, mindless nonsense?

Sergei   Hey! – old fellow – I've had a hard time of it, these last years. If it wasn't for Tania and the children, I'd have killed myself. Yes, I tell you now, I've thought many times about ending it all –

Kolia   – Keep the money. It's a gift. That's all you're getting from me. You're worthless, depressing company – and you're a bore.

Sergei   Me? A *bore*? Have you any idea how insulting that is? How little you know me! How little you know me!

Sergei *gets to his feet and takes off his jacket. He pauses, unsteadily, brimming with self-righteous drunken anger.*

Kolia   What an earth are you doing?

Sergei   Doing? I'm going to give you a thrashing. A damn good hiding, that's what. Step outside.

Kolia   Don't be ridiculous.

Sergei *has left the veranda and raises his fists.*

Sergei   So I'm ridiculous now, am I? A "ridiculous bore". That's how you'd describe me to your smart Moscow friends. Well – to hell with them! See how you like being punched in the face by a ridiculous bore!

Kolia *has stepped tiredly down off the veranda and into the garden.* **Sergei** *circles him, making little feints and jabs.*

Kolia   Calm down – sit down. You're making a complete fool of yourself.

Sergei   You come down here, you accept my hospitality and yet all you do is pour insults on my head! Put your fists up, man! Defend yourself!

He takes a swing at **Kolia** *who effortlessly steps out of the way.*

Kolia   I've just given you two hundred roubles, for god's sake.

Sergei   That has nothing to do with it.

He takes another swing, and another, unsteady on his feet. **Kolia** *steps out of the way, easily. Then* **Sergei** *charges him, swings at him – misses. Recovers himself, sways dramatically.*

Kolia   This is absurd.

Kolia *steps forward, delivers a crisp professional punch that hits* **Sergei** *on the nose. He crumples immediately to the ground.* **Kolia** *steps back.* **Sergei** *gets to his knees. His nose is bleeding.* **Kolia** *goes and gets his jacket.*

Sergei   Congratulations. You've drawn blood. You've probably broken my nose. I hope you're satisfied.

Kolia   Get to bed and sober up.

Sergei *stands. Looks disbelievingly at the blood on his fingers.* **Kolia** *hands him his jacket.* **Sergei** *takes it.*

Kolia   Off to bed, there's a good fellow.

Sergei (*voice cracking*)   I called you my "friend". Yet how little you know me! You're no longer my friend!

Sergei *weaves away.* **Kolia** *shouts after him.*

Kolia   Good! Excellent. The best news I've had in a long time!

Kolia *stands there: incredulous, angry, hugely frustrated, and deeply worried by the "brother-in-law" appellation. He goes back inside the summer house. Slams the door angrily.*

Act Two

Scene One

Dusk. Some days later.

The summer house is transformed. Everything has been painted as new in rather horrible, garish colours. The uprights on the balustrade have been picked out in alternate black and white. Bunting has been draped all over and coloured lanterns have been hung from every projection. **Radish**, *on the roof, strings the last lengths of bunting.*

The tables have been covered with cloths and here and there punch bowls and ranked glasses are set out.

Varia *and* **Kolia** *wander in. They are dressed for the party, smart.*

Varia *is made up: she looks beautiful, different, somehow.* **Varia** *lights a cigarette.*

Kolia   Well, you see – it's certainly different . . . Very bright.

Varia   Yes, just think – a few days ago when you arrived you said: "nothing has changed. Everything exactly as it used to be" . . .

Kolia   But that's what I felt. It was as if nothing had happened in the last ten years.

Varia   And how quickly everything can change . . . (*snaps fingers*) Change forever . . . (*pause*) You know the bailiffs have been.

Kolia   Yes, yes.

Varia   And Dolzhikov has offered to buy the estate. The whole thing.

Kolia   My god! What does Sergei say?

Varia   What do you think? He's absolutely delighted. Dolzhikov will own the estate and Sergei will stay on as estate manager – on a salary. Not princely, but a salary, all the same.

Kolia   Sergei? Estate manager? I thought Dolzhikov was smart.

Varia   Oh, he's very smart. Sergei and the family are now going to move here, into the summer house. Kleopatra Dolzhikova and her beau are going to live in the big house. Whenever they're married.

Kolia   My god. And Sergei's not bothered?

Varia   He's extremely happy. He thinks he's pulled a fast one. His debts are cleared, he has a salary for the first time in his life and he still lives on the estate. Not quite in the same style, to be sure – No, he's like a little boy locked in the sweetshop.

Kolia   And what do *you* think, Varia?

Varia (*looks at him*)   "All things pass".

Kolia (*irritated suddenly*)   Yes, yes . . . I can see you women talk together all the time. You've been talking to Natasha.

Varia   What else do you expect us to do? You men are endlessly fascinating – the way you behave, your peculiar philosophies of life. We'd have no conversation if you didn't provide us with so much substance.

Kolia   Well, I'll be gone soon. One less man to talk about.

Varia   Oh, but we'll still talk about you, Kolia, even when you're not here. There's no respite, I'm afraid.

(*Slight pause.*) What happened the other evening with Sergei? Did you have a fight? He won't tell us.

Kolia   He was drunk. He borrowed money off me, two hundred roubles – all the while telling me he was an "idealist". I lost patience and then he took offence, challenged me to a boxing match and I punched him in the nose.

Varia (*delighted*)   How I would have loved to see that! How can we *not* talk about you – you men. It's endlessly amusing.

Kolia *has to smile.*

Kolia   Yes, well, we're a poor lot, I admit . . . A poor lot . . . How is Sergei?

Varia   He was a bit subdued for a while. Very theatrically melancholy. Lots of heavy sighs . . . To be honest I think his memory's more or less a complete and utter blank. That's the advantage about drinking too much: the past is a blur – everything goes.

Kolia   Yes, well, I should probably apologise, I suppose . . .

(*He takes her hand.*) And what about you, Varia? What will you do when the estate is sold?

Varia *enjoys* **Kolia** *holding her hand.*

Varia   What I've always done. I have my job. I'm a doctor – and there's never going to be a shortage of sick people. Tania is my oldest friend. I love the family, the girls . . . I'll come and visit, I'll smoke too many cigarettes and slowly pine away . . .

Kolia   Pine away. Nonsense! Why should you pine away? You're the most intelligent, bravest person I know.

She looks at him: don't you know? Her gaze seems to say. Are you really that blind?

Varia   Dear Kolia . . . Maybe I'll come to Moscow and pay you a visit.

Kolia   That would be wonderful.

Varia   Yes, wouldn't it . . .

She stands up. Their hands separate.

A couple of musicians arrive, one with an accordion, the other with a violin in its case. They go into the summer house.

Varia   Shall we go and find the others?

Kolia   Yes – I think I need a drink. Something stronger than punch.

Varia   Prepare ourselves for the "betrothal ball".

They wander off, chuckling.

Kolia   You know: I'm actually quite pleased Sergei has no memory of that night. It would be too embarrassing, otherwise. I couldn't look him in the eye – his idealist's eye . . .

They laugh together. A shared joke. A shared sensibility.

Radish *has strung the last of the bunting. He disappears around the back of the roof.*

The lights dim.

Scene Two

Night approaches.

And the multi-coloured lanterns glow and the windows shine from the lights on inside. The new paint gleams. The sound of music – an accordion and a fiddle – laughter and conversation swell from indoors.

Sergei *and* **Tania** *enter, followed by* **Natasha**. *All dressed in white like figures from some ancient photograph.* **Natasha** *looks ravishingly beautiful, eyes dark with kohl – a beautiful woman, suddenly. They all stop at the very edge of the stage looking at the summer house, taking it in for a moment or two. Before –*

The summer house door bursts open and **Dolzhikov** *emerges. Dressed to the vulgar nines.*

Dolzhikov (*shouting back inside*)   Louder, damn you! I can't hear a thing. It's not a wake, you know!

The music gets louder.

Dolzhikov Kleopatra!

Kleopatra and Misail emerge from the other door. Kleopatra is extravagantly done up: plunging neckline, complicated hair style. Misail looks very uncomfortable in a too large pale grey suit.

Dolzhikov Come here.

He holds his arms out. Kleopatra steps into them. They begin to dance.

Dolzhikov Can you hear the music?

Kleopatra Not really.

Dolzhikov *Louder*, damn your eyes!

The music gets louder, more manic. Another violin kicks in, a tambourine. A surging polka. Dolzhikov, enjoying dancing with his daughter, sweeps her along the veranda – Misail recoiling – and off onto the lawn. They swirl and turn through the tables. The onlookers freeze.

Dolzhikov (*shouting*) That's more like it. Faster! Louder! Are you happy, my darling?

Kleopatra (*shouting back*) I'm the happiest girl in Dubechnia, Father. No, I'm the happiest girl in Russia!

Dolzhikov Then I'm the happiest man in the world! The whole grand wonderful magnificent wide world!

He laughs, intoxicated. They surge around the stage to the rhythms of the polka oblivious to the onlookers.

Dolzhikov (*bellowing*) Faster! Louder!

Kleopatra (*shouting*) Louder! Faster!

She laughs wildly, exhilarated. The music obliges. They swing back onto the verandah. Misail holds open the door and they dance back inside. Misail follows.

A final chord and the music crashes to a halt. Silence.

Tania *bursts into tears. She runs to* **Natasha** *who hugs her.*

Natasha   We must be brave, darling.

Tania   It's too awful. Horrible . . . Look at Kolia's summer house – (*To* **Sergei**, *furious.*) What have you done? Look at your handiwork! Are you satisfied? This is our new "home".

Do you know what it means to me to lose this estate? It's been in my family for generations –

Sergei   – I didn't do it to you, my dear. I keep telling you: circumstances did this to you, events beyond our control. Fate did this to us. Le Destin.

Tania   How can you say this to me? I have to live like some provincial housewife because of your Japanese investments. It's . . . shocking, unbearable.

She bursts into tears again.

Inside a gentler waltz strikes up. **Natasha** *holds her.*

Sergei   Don't be so melodramatic. You'll get used to it. The children are thrilled. They love the summer house.

Tania   I loved the summer house – but not this . . . this monstrosity.

Sergei   I think it's perfectly charming. Now – where's the punch? I think a glass of punch would help us all.

He wanders over to the punch bowl. **Natasha** *helps* **Tania** *dry her eyes, generally compose herself.*

Natasha   Just try to be calm. Give it sometime. Let things run their natural course – it's what you always tell me.

Sergei, *wholly unmoved and unconcerned, pours himself a liberal glassful.*

Dolzhikov *steps out onto the veranda. Cigar on the go.*

Sergei   I know we're going to love it here. We spend more time at the summer house than we do the main house, anyway – we're never away from the summer house . . .

No, no, I won't hear this moaning and wailing. Won't hear it. Jamais de ma vie! This is the best thing that's ever happened to our family.

(*Sees* **Dolzhikov**.) My dear friend! Vladimir. Come, I don't think you've met my wife.

He comes out to meet **Tania**. *She exudes a soul-shrivelling arctic chill but* **Dolzikhov** *doesn't notice.*

Dolzhikov   My dear, Madame Losev, an intense and profound pleasure . . . (*kisses her hand*) I can't tell you how happy we all are that things should have turned out so perfect. So tip-top.

Sergei   Exactly. Tip-top. Everything for the best in the best of all –

Tania   – Please! Sergei . . . You know I detest that expression.

Sergei   My sister-in-law – Miss Natasha.

Dolzhikov (*to* **Natasha**)   Completely, utterly enchanted, I am sure, Madame-moyselle . . .

Sergei   Très bien, formidable!

Dolzhikov (*to* **Tania**)   Come inside, Madame, dear Madame. We have champagne on ice, caviar, white salmon, roll-mops, tangerines . . .

He offers her his arm. She does not take it.

Tania   I'm not in the least bit hungry.

Dolzhikov   Then help yourself as the mood takes you, my dear, delightful lady. Let me have a plate of titbits brought out to you.

He draws **Sergei** *aside. His tone changes.*

Dolzhikov   I thought you said we were getting an orchestra. And what do we have? Two fiddlers and an accordion. This is my daughter getting betrothed, here.

Sergei   I'm as annoyed as you are, Vladimir. I was promised a full orchestra. Outrageous.

Dolzhikov   Well you get that fifty roubles back from them. Daylight robbery.

Sergei   Leave it to me, old chap.

He taps the side of his nose.

Dolzhikov *goes back into the summer house.*

Sergei   Charming fellow. Rough diamond, true – but there's more than meets the eye. Try to be a tiny bit civil, Tania – it won't kill you.

Tania   It *will* kill me! The sheer vulgarity! –

Natasha   – Have a glass of punch, dear.

As she busies herself at the punchbowl **Sergei** *goes back into the summer house, passing* **Kleopatra** *and* **Misail** *as they wander out.* **Kleopatra** *is a bit drunk by now. She tries to straighten* **Misail**'s *tie, adjust his jacket.*

Kleopatra   What possessed you to buy this suit? You look like you just got out of prison –

Misail   – It was the cheapest I could find.

Kleopatra   You don't need to save money. You're my betrothed, silly. Give me a kiss.

She kisses him briefly but passionately. Breaks apart.

Tania   I can't believe my eyes. Is that the strumpet who's going to be living in my house? Let the earth open, swallow me up!

Natasha   Have some punch, darling. Turn away – ignore her.

Tania   The shame. I'll never forgive Sergei. Never!

Back on the veranda.

Kleopatra   How I love you. In fact how I love your horrible suit. Only buy cheap suits, my darling. Never change. Show them you don't give a tuppenny damn –

She tries to kiss him again. But he recoils.

Kleopatra   What's wrong?

Misail   I think I had too much champagne. Indigestion . . . Give me a minute or two.

A waltz strikes up.

Kleopatra   Right. Next dance. Get your energy back. Is your father here?

Misail   No, he, ah, refused to come. He's disowned me.

Kleopatra   Good. More fool him, then. See you in two minutes.

She goes back in.

Misail *leans on the balustrade. He looks like he might vomit. He sees* **Natasha**, *smiles, straightens, very happy to see her.*

Misail   Good evening. Thank you so much for coming.

Natasha *wanders over, they shake hands,* **Misail** *gives a small bow.*

Natasha   We've met before, haven't we?

Misail   Yes. I'm amazed you remember.

Natasha   It was at the town hall. You won the gold medal for poetry.

Misail   A long time ago.

Natasha   I remember your poem so well – so heartfelt, so moving. What was it called?

Misail   "Midnight" . . .

Tania (*calling*)   Natasha . . .

Natasha   Excuse me.

She wanders off. He looks after her, utterly entranced. **Radish** *comes through the garden at the side. Looks at him with some concern.*

Radish   Psst . . . Misail . . . Are you all right?

Misail   Radish . . . Thank god you came. Come in. Have a drink.

Radish   I'm not coming in . . . No, no. I wouldn't be seen dead in there. But I'll drink your health, certainly.

Misail *helps* **Radish** *to some punch. They move to one side.* **Natasha** *is still trying to console* **Tania**. **Radish** *toasts.*

Radish   To your marriage. To your happy marriage.

Misail (*full of doubt*)   What? Oh, that, yes . . . Thank you. Very kind . . .

Radish   Aren't you drinking? You'll need drink to cope with that girl, my boy. She'd take on a squadron of dragoons, that one.

Misail   I feel a terrible nausea, all of a sudden – In fact I've felt sick since we finished painting the summer house. I don't know what's happening to me –

Radish   – It's just nerves. I felt nervous when I got betrothed.

Misail   I never knew you had a wife.

Radish   I don't. She's dead. Typhus took her – and my two boys.

Misail   Oh. I'm sorry. Terribly sorry . . . that's awful . . . How come I never asked you about your family? . . . Shameful of me . . . Maybe I will have a drink.

He goes over to the punch bowl and pours himself a glass. He sees **Tania** *and* **Natasha** *– smiles at them, gives a little bow.*

Natasha   I forgot to say congratulations. Your fiancée looks very beautiful.

Misail (*struck by* **Natasha**'s *beauty again*)   Oh, yes, thank you
. . . very kind . . . Yes . . .

Natasha   I suspect we'll be seeing more of each other.

Misail   Really? I very much hope so –

Natasha   – Now we're to be neighbours.

Misail   Yes . . . Yes, of course. That would be wonderf –
most agreeable.

Natasha   Don't let me keep you from your friend.

Misail   Thank you . . . very kind.

Natasha   Thank you.

Misail *goes back to* **Radish**. *Throwing a troubled glance back at*
Natasha.

Misail   What should I do, Radish? I'm beginning to think
of running away. I don't know what I've got myself into.
Kleopatra – she keeps talking about children, the estate, how
we'll improve it, make it flourish, our children's
"patrimony". All I wanted was to work with my hands. How
did I end up like this in a . . . a horrible suit, at my betrothal
party, to be married to the richest girl in Dubechnia
province? How did it happen?

Radish   Life has a funny way of diverting you from your
chosen road.

Misail   What should I do?

Radish (*baffled*)   Do what you want to do. Go your own way.
You know my motto: lice eat grass, rust eats iron –

Misail   – Lies eat the soul . . . Yes . . . Good god . . .

He groans and sits down.

Misail   "Lies eat the soul" – that's it, that's it!

Dolzhikov *stomps out onto the terrace.*

Dolzhikov Misail! Hoi! She wants you. Dancing. Now! What's up with you? Try to look a bit merrier, sonny, will you? Look like you're under sentence of death.

Misail *goes in.* **Dolzhikov** *wanders down to confront* **Radish**.

Dolzhikov What're you doing here?

Radish I came to pay my respects, to the bride and groom – and the happy father, of course.

(*Raises glass.*) And to pick up my ladder. I forgot it.

Dolzhikov Well, pick it up tomorrow. I don't want people wandering around the grounds carrying ladders on an evening like this.

Radish I'll pick it up tomorrow. Or the next day. One day soon, anyway.

Dolzhikov And Misail's not working for you no more, right? You're not filling his head with your damned nonsense. I've heard you. "Life is like a carrot" – Rubbish! You might as well say life is like . . . a corn-cob, a feather duster. Stuff and nonsense.

Radish Whatever you say, sir. You're the boss.

They look at each other. **Radish** *doesn't flinch.*

Dolzhikov Have another drink and be off with you.

Radish You're very generous. Thank you.

Dolzhikov *heads back inside.* **Radish** *pours himself another drink.*

Varia *and* **Kolia** *wander on stage, arm in arm.* **Varia**, *in her quiet way, loving the close contact.*

Kolia I suppose we'd better go in.

Varia Yes. Look, I'll go and console Tania.

Kolia I just hope Sergei doesn't get drunk.

Varia   Oh, he's bound to get drunk. That's the one thing we can be sure of this evening.

Kolia   Where is he?

He goes into the summer house. Passing **Dolzhikov** *who is emerging with a plate of sweetmeats for* **Tania**. *They nod good evening.*

Varia *heading for* **Tania**, *sees* **Radish**.

Radish   Evening, Mam.

Varia   Good evening, Radish.

Radish   You know me, do you?

Varia   You did some work at the hospital. I'm a doctor there.

Radish   Oh, yes. I remember you. The lady doctor, of course.

Dolzikhov *approaches* **Tania**, *thrusts the plate at her.*

Dolzhikov   My dear Madame Losev, have a nibble at these can-apes. Delicious. Mushroom vol-au-vents, cod roe on toast, Polish sausage.

Tania (*reeling*)   Most kind. I couldn't eat a thing.

Dolzhikov   What about you, jolly mad'moyselle.

Natasha   Thank you so much, but no.

Dolzhikov   Then I shall go in search of hungrier folk. You ladies with your diets! If you feel peckish we've loads of grub inside.

He wanders back in, munching a vol-au-vent. **Tania** *watches him go, horror-struck.*

Varia *finishes her conversation with* **Radish** *and wanders over to* **Tania** *and* **Natasha**. **Tania** *reaches out her hand for her.*

Tania   I can't speak. My heart is broken.

Varia   There, there, this is the worst moment. You'll adjust, it won't seem so bad.

Natasha   Precisely, let things run their course.

Tania   You both sound exactly like Kolia – where is he, anyway?

Varia   Gone to look for Sergei.

Tania   Look for the vodka, that's where he'll be.

Kolia *comes out of the summer house, gripping the arm of a rather unsteady* **Sergei***. They head for the women.* **Radish** *looking on.*

Sergei   Ah, ma très belle petite femme.

Tania   Don't ever use any term of endearment to me again, in any language, whatsoever!

Sergei   Now, now – allez doucement – you can't loiter out here all night. You must come in and meet the bride to be. Dolzhikov is very keen that you become acquainted.

Tania   Dolzhikov? Is that man to rule our lives forever?

Natasha   Let's go in and get it over with.

Tania   I do it with bad grace – bad grace, I tell you.

Sergei   Nonsense – you can charm the birds out of the trees.

He offers her his arm and she takes it. They go in, followed by **Natasha***.*

Varia *and* **Kolia** *move to one side and sit as far away from the summer house as possible. They sit down.*

Kolia   We have to go in ourselves, for a minute or two. If only for Tania's sake.

Varia   Yes . . . But let them get acquainted first.

On the veranda **Kleopatra** *appears, looking for* **Misail***. She sees* **Radish***, draining his punch glass.*

Kleopatra   Hoi! You – What're you doing here?

Radish   I came to drink your health, Miss.

Kleopatra   But you weren't invited –

Radish   – Misail invited me.

Kleopatra   You're not to call him Misail any more, do you understand?

He's Mr Poloznev to you, from now on. Got that? Show some respect.

Radish (*unperturbed*)   Oh no. He won't stand for that.

Kleopatra   What're you talking about? I order you to call him Mr Poloznev.

Radish   You can order till you're blue in the face, Miss Kleopatra. Misail will always want me to call him "Misail" – will good old Misail.

Kleopatra   Get out of here before I summon my father.

Radish (*raises glass*)   I wish you every happiness. You – and especially *Misail*.

He drains glass and wanders away.

Kleopatra *stomps inside calling, "Misail? Misail where are you?" The music strikes up again, another waltz.*

Over on their bench **Varia** *stands up. She begins to sway to the music.*

Varia   How I love this tune . . . Perhaps we should have a dance, Kolia . . .

Kolia   Oh, my dancing days are over.

Varia   You danced with Natasha.

Kolia   She can be very insistent. Dancing is for the young.

Varia   What nonsense you talk. Dancing is for those who wish to dance. As simple as that.

Varia *sways to and fro, turns, holding her hands out as if dancing with an invisible partner. It's making* **Kolia** *uncomfortable.* **Varia** *suddenly stops. She goes and sits down beside him again. She takes his hand.*

Varia   Kolia, would you do me a favour?

Kolia   Of course. Anything.

Varia   Would you kiss me – on the lips?

Kolia *is stunned.*

Kolia   Kiss you?

Varia   Yes . . . Please. On the lips.

Kolia   On the lips, you say?

Varia   Just once, on the lips, only for a second or two.

Kolia   But why?

Varia (*pause*)   I want to have something to remember.

Pause.

Kolia   Well, it's most odd . . . But, if you want. Of course . . . (*pause*) I feel a bit embarrassed, Varia.

Varia   Just do it . . . I won't bite . . . Kiss me. On the lips . . .

They begin to move their heads together slowly, preparing to kiss. Closer, closer. Suddenly –

Natasha's Voice   Kolia!

Kolia *jerks back from* **Varia**. **Varia** *holds her head in position for a second, her mouth parted, her eyes closed, frozen.*

Natasha *runs out onto the veranda.*

Natasha   Kolia! Quickly . . . Sergei's fallen over! He's much drunker than we thought! Tania said you've got to come now!

Natasha *comes out to them.* **Varia** *smiles, her eyes still closed.* **Kolia** *seizes his opportunity. Leaps to his feet.*

Kolia   I'll be right there.

He and **Natasha** *dash into the summer house.*

Varia *takes this huge blow with stoic resignation.*

She stands up. Thinking. Standing still for a moment, composing herself. She stands there alone.

Then **Sergei**, *held up by* **Kolia**, *stumbles out from the summer house.* **Kolia** *leads him to the side, to a flowerbed. He falls to his knees and vomits.* **Kolia** *checks – hopes no one's looking.*

Tania *and* **Natasha** *come out of the summer house. Spot* **Sergei** *and* **Kolia**. *Rush over, concerned.* **Varia** *runs over.* **Kolia** *steps back and he and* **Natasha** *look on. A lone accordion is playing in the summer house, the gaiety has died down.* **Varia** *and* **Tania** *haul* **Sergei** *to his feet.*

Kolia   How is he?

Tania   Extremely bad, I'm glad to say. He should have a good two days of real misery with a bit of luck . . . We'd better get him home. Thank god we didn't bring the girls.

(*Berating* **Sergei**.) What do you imagine they'd think of you, their father, drunk on vodka like a peasant!

Kolia   Do you need any help?

Sergei   Aidez-moi! Kolia, mon cher ami . . .

Tania   Come along, Varia, take an arm.

They both hoist **Sergei** *up and lead him off.*

Varia   Good night, Kolia.

Tania   Good night, and my apologies. For everything.

Kolia   See you tomorrow.

Natasha *lingers.* **Misail** *comes out onto the veranda, watches her and* **Kolia**, *unseen.*

Natasha   I should go back with them. See if I can do anything . . .

Kolia   Yes . . . (*Looks round.*) It's winding up here.

Natasha   It's still early. I'll just make sure they're all right . . . Perhaps I could come back –

Kolia   – What?

Natasha   Have some hot chocolate, or something, a coffee, finish off the champagne. I felt I hardly saw you this evening, hardly spoke to you.

Kolia   Sergei . . . What can you do with him? I had to stay close . . .

Natasha   Of course . . . I'll see you in a little while, then. When everyone's gone . . .

Kolia   Right . . . See you later . . .

Natasha *slips away.* **Kolia** *turns. A couple of musicians with their instruments come down the steps and head off into the darkness.*

Misail *follows.* **Kolia** *pauses.*

Misail   Ah, it's you, sir.

Kolia   Congratulations. Most enjoyable party.

Misail   I hope it's the last one I ever go to. I'll look after this estate, sir. I assure you I'll do my best.

Kolia   Good. Excellent. It's a lovely place.

Misail   You know it well?

Kolia   I spent many years of my boyhood here. I was an old friend of the family . . . Anyway – (*offers hand*) Good luck to you.

He and **Misail** *shake hands.*

Misail   Sir, there was one thing I'd like to ask, if you don't mind . . . As a man of the world, a man of experience.

Kolia   Of course . . .

Misail   Do you believe in "love at first sight"?

Kolia   I've never experienced it, but I have heard it can happen.

Misail   How should one act upon it – if one experiences it? . . .

Kolia   I've no idea . . . Maybe you should be true to yourself . . . (*They look at each other.*) This has happened to you, I suppose . . .

Misail   Yes, yes it has. And I find myself somewhat . . . overwhelmed and confused.

Kleopatra (*shouting, off*)   – MISAIL! Where in god's name are you? We can't wait all night!

Misail   My fiancée . . . Waiting in the carriage . . . I'd better go . . .

Kolia   You're a lucky man. Congratulations.

Misail *shakes* **Kolia**'s *hand fervently.*

Misail   Thank you for your advice, sir.

He slips away. **Kolia** *watches him leave, mystified, then goes into the summer house.*

Moonshadows flit across the garden and the summer house.

Olga *comes on stage, moves around the veranda collecting some scattered glasses.*

She leaves.

Kolia, *in his shirtsleeves, steps out onto the veranda with a drink in his hand. Takes a sip. Listens to the night noises – the crickets, the owls, the frogs croaking.*

He puts his drink down and steps down in to the garden,wandering about. Suddenly –

Natasha (*whispering*)   Kolia?

Kolia *freezes. He puts down his glass and steps into shadow.*

Natasha *advances. Her hair is down, she has a shawl around her shoulders. She looks like she's wearing nightclothes. She approaches the veranda.*

Natasha   Kolia? It's me. I've come. They're all asleep . . . (*Going up the steps.*) They don't know I'm here . . . I crept away, didn't make a sound . . . Kolia?

Kolia *moves carefully deeper into the garden, keeping to the shadows.*

Natasha *goes into the summer house.*

Kolia, *in some panic, searches for a perfect hiding place. He crouches down out of sight. The light goes on in the dormer window. Is turned down. After a little time* **Natasha** *emerges.*

Natasha   Kolia, are you there? . . . It's me, Natasha . . . I've come, like we said . . . Kolia?

Suddenly, **Natasha** *notices the glass. It's half drunk. She holds it up. Looks out into the garden.*

Natasha   Kolia . . . I know you're there . . . Why are you hiding? Why are you hiding from me? Kolia, don't do this to me . . .

Kolia *shrinks deeper in his shadow.* **Natasha** *realises what's happening. She tries not to cry.*

Natasha   I'm sorry, Kolia. I'm so sorry!

She runs off. Silence. **Kolia** *straightens himself up. Very cautiously he approaches the summer house. Checks there's no one there – goes in. A light goes on in the dormer window. Then the lights die down in the summer house.*

The lights change.

Scene Two

A grey, dawn light. A few birds begin to sing. A mist drifts through the garden.

The door to the summer house opens. **Kolia** *appears. He's in his travelling coat and hat. He has his leather grip in his hand.*

Quietly, carefully, he positions a note as visibly as possible on the veranda table. And then he creeps away through the garden in the opposite direction from the big house.

Lights dim to black.

Scene Three

It's afternoon. Some days later.

The summer house still looks garish, newly painted and vulgar, but we've almost grown accustomed to the Chinese lanterns and the bunting. **Radish**'s *ladder is still propped against the eaves.*

On the veranda, **Tania**, **Varia** *and* **Natasha** *sit.* **Varia** *smoking.* **Tania** *sewing,* **Natasha** *reading.*

In front of the house, **Sergei** – *in suitable squirearchical country gear is talking to* **Misail**, *also dressed – uncomfortably – like a country landowner.*

Misail   – I don't understand: I offered them ten roubles but they refused to work. That's twice their usual rate.

Sergei   That's because they're peasants. Now, if you offered them three buckets of vodka, they'd be in the fields until sundown.

Misail   But it makes no sense. For ten roubles they could buy thirty buckets of vodka.

Sergei   No, no, no. My dear, Misail . . . You've got a lot to learn. They don't think like that. They don't think like you and me. They're peasants.

Misail   It just doesn't seem right somehow. We're cheating them –

Sergei   – They'll cheat you, give them half a chance. Rob you blind. You can't treat them with fairness – they'll think you're soft in the head.

Sergei *leaves.* **Natasha** *looks up, comes over to greet* **Misail**. **Misail** *removes a manuscript from his jacket. Offers it.*

Natasha   Hello . . . What's this?

Misail   It's my poem – "Midnight".

Natasha (*taking it*)   Why thank you . . .

She smiles at him, genuinely pleased. **Misail**'*s heart spins.*

Misail   I've written a new verse . . . I think you might find it interesting. At the end of the poem.

Natasha   How intriguing. I look forward to it . . . Thank you, Misail . . .

Misail   I'd better go and meet Mr Losev. Perhaps we could talk about the poem, another time . . .

Natasha   That would be very nice. I'd love to . . .

Misail *leaves.* **Natasha** *rejoins the others, leafing through the manuscript.*

Tania   What's that?

Natasha   It's a poem Misail wrote.

She sits down and begins to read.

Varia *puts her cigarette out.*

Varia   He seems quite happy, Sergei. Happy being the estate manager, happy living in the summer house. Happy with his life . . .

Tania (*holding up a small smock*)   Never happier . . . Who would have thought I'd be sewing my own children's clothes? My mother would have had a fit and died on the spot if she'd ever seen this.

Varia   Times change, everything changes . . . All things pass.

Tania (*not listening*)   Now let's see if it actually fits Ekaterina. The acid test.

Varia   I should go to the station – my train's due. I'll get my bag.

They both go into the summer house. Call of "Ekaterina?" "Darling, where are you?"

Natasha *sits on reading* **Misail**'s *poem. She comes to the last page of the manuscript. Her concentration increases as she reads the final verse. She's overcome, can't believe what she's reading. Suddenly she begins to cry. Sobs briefly. Controls herself. Holds the manuscript tightly and goes quickly inside.*

Pause. Birdsong.

Varia *comes out of the house. She's in a coat and has her big doctor's bag in her hand, clearly about to leave. She pauses, looks back at the summer house, looks up at* **Kolia**'s *room.*

Then **Kolia** *appears from around the side of the house wearing his formal dark suit.*

Just for an instant we might think he's returned – but **Varia**'s *complete lack of reaction lets us know that there is a blending of space and time going on here. Or indeed that we are witnessing some wishful projection of* **Varia**'s, *some brief fantasy she's indulging in.* **Kolia** *is not by the summer house – he's in his office in Moscow. A fact made unequivocally clear when, behind him, note book and pencil in hand, appears his middle-aged secretary* **Mrs Luganovitch**.

Kolia *is giving dictation.*

Kolia   . . . And I would be grateful if you could respond to this communication with the most urgent despatch . . . I remain, dear sir, yours etcetera etcetera . . .

Mrs Luganovitch *takes this down.*

Varia *takes a step towards him. And* **Kolia** *turns.* **Varia** *half-raises her hand – and* **Kolia** *stiffens, as if somehow being physically affected by her movements.*

Mrs Luganovitch   Will that be everything, sir?

Kolia   What? . . . No . . . Mrs Luganovitch . . . I want you to book me a seat on a train, right away. I want to leave this afternoon.

Mrs Luganovitch   To St Petersburg?

Kolia   No . . . To Dubechnia.

Mrs Luganovitch   Dubechnia? Certainly, sir. Right away. I think there's one leaves at four.

Kolia *stands still thinking.*

Varia *stands there, begins to button her coat, staring at* **Kolia**.

Mrs Luganovitch   It's not an express, I'm afraid.

Kolia   That's not important. It's just . . . You see, I have a friend there – an old friend, a . . . yes, a *dear* friend – and I think she would like to see me . . . Rather, I would like to see her. I need to see her . . .

He seems to be looking directly at **Varia**.

Kolia   You know how it is . . . Sometimes you just don't . . . At a given moment . . . You need time . . .

Varia *steps off the veranda and looks back at the transformed summer house.*

Mrs Luganovitch *doesn't know what her boss is talking about.*

Mrs Luganovitch   Of course . . . Shall I go ahead and book the ticket? The four o'clock train?

Varia *seems to be looking up at* **Kolia**'s *window,* **Kolia**'s *room. Then she turns away, turning her back on* **Kolia**, *as if she's realised this is all wishful thinking and her* **Kolia** *would never behave like this.*

Kolia *doesn't know what to do.*

Kolia   Ah . . . No . . . No . . . Actually, no, don't bother. No
. . . I'm a bit busy here. There's a lot on . . . Maybe I'll go
next week. Yes, next week. Leave it . . . Makes more sense
. . . To go next week . . .

Mrs Luganovitch   Whatever you decide, sir.

Kolia   Yes.. Next week would make much more sense.

She smiles, leaves.

Kolia *stands for a moment, as if his mind is racing incontradictory
directions, held in an agonising stasis of indecision – and then,
slowly, he leaves the stage.*

Varia *– alone – stands there for a moment, thinking. Then she
smiles. Then she picks up her bag and walks away. A beat. Birdsong.*

Radish *comes in. Goes to his ladder. Picks it off the wall and carries
it away.*

Lights dim to black.

The end.